Find Your Nicne
As A
Professional
Photographer

A Guide To Dominating
Your Market

Find Your Niche As A Professional Photographer

A Guide To Dominating Your Market

James Michael

Zelfin

Find Your Niche As A Professional Photographer

A Guide To Dominating Your Market

Zelfin

Suite 302

3100 Five Forks Trickum Road

Lilburn GA 30047

Published in the United States of America

by Zelfin LLC

Cover design and photography courtesy of

J Michael

Michael, James

Find Your Niche In Professional Photography

ISBN 978-0-9997669-3-4

Contents

1. Reality Check

Are You Sure About This?

It seems inevitable that a new photographer who pours a large amount of money into his new hobby soon begins pondering a move from photography as a hobby to photography as a business. It might appear reasonable to try to recoup the sizable investment in camera bodies, lenses, and other accoutrements by offering photographic services. Perhaps you find yourself in the same boat, perhaps at the behest of a friend or relative who asks you to shoot their wedding or a portrait. The business of photography might appear lucrative and easy to the uninitiated. This illusion is soon dispelled when the reality of the true world of the professional photographer is unveiled. I would caution you to carefully consider your decision to enter the field before fully committing. Don't quit your day job just yet. In this chapter we will explain some of the risks and realities associated with the profession and begin to formulate a strategy to manage those risks and minimize their impact.

Photography saw an explosion of interest in the 1960s partly as a result of the film Blowup, which portrayed a playboy photographer with hot models competing for his attention. And thus was born the concept of photography as a glamour profession. Another contributing factor was the increase in mass production efficiencies and technical achievements that made photography for the masses possible via the Instamatic and Polaroid cameras advertised in the 1960s through the 1980s. Ansel Adams' brilliant images gave birth to a generation of nature photographers that continues today.

The digital photography revolution we are now seeing seems to have sparked yet another resurgence of interest in photography, and along with it another wave of would-be professional photographers. Social media makes it easy for these photographers to distribute their images. The gratifying instant feedback in the form of "great capture!" provides the little encouragement they need to jump from the hobbyist level to the professional level. Most fail to realize that the consequences for failure are much higher for professional photographers than amateurs. Failure for amateurs is somewhat expected, whereas failure at the professional level can be devastating to a career, or worse. An amateur who takes a few photos at a friend's wedding is unlikely to be sued when the photos don't turn out so great. Some might believe, in addition to the monetary aspects, that the distinction between an amateur and a professional is found in owning so-called "pro" equipment. The popularity of prosumer photographic gear would tend to support that perspective. However most of the amateur equipment today is of such high quality and capability as to allow one to compete on a quality basis with those pros who have much greater investments in their tools. Professional grade equipment offers more in terms of reliability and performance. No, the real distinction between amateur and professional photographers is that the professional is able to consistently produce excellent images, on time and on budget. The professional photographer must do this under often difficult circumstances, with uncooperative subjects, and in unexpected conditions.

Glamour Professions

There are a number of glamour professions that always seem to attract those willing to work for small change. These include those working as TV anchors, models, actors, and photographers. Very few of the folks working in these roles receive adequate remuneration for their work in the form of a living wage. For every successful photographer there may be a hundred or more barely making a living pursuing their dream, if that. If you are intent on pursuing photography as a profession then it is important to be aware of the implications of doing so. If you make the decision to proceed, it will be up to you to determine your course of action, whether to join the 99% or become one of the 1% who excels in the photographic profession.

Why is the ratio of unsuccessful to successful photographers so high? There are a number of factors that come into play. First of all it seems deceptively simple to start up and run a photography business. You just need to hand out a few business cards, create a web page, take a few phone calls, shoot a few exotic models, and send a bill, right? It appears easy but it's not. Many who decide to go down this path do little in the way of preparation and planning. They fail to create a business plan and fail to develop their expertise in a single area or genre of photography. They may be unaware how important it is to develop relationships and contacts within the markets they intend to serve. They may become too focused on equipment and believe that one must be equipped for every variety of possible assignments. As a result they may spend more time looking for and buying equipment than developing their portfolio. A common sight at many events is a photographer who looks like he is ready for a safari loaded down with equipment. After all, he needs to *appear professional*, right? He may squander financial resources on equipment that he will rarely if ever use. Despite the increasing ability to rent all sorts of camera equipment there is often a resistance to do so.

If photographers were more inclined to become proficient with the equipment that they have and use that equipment to learn to excel in a particular genre of photography they would be much more likely to achieve success than they would by spending time and money on yet more equipment.

Photographers are like other entrepreneurs and tend to see business opportunities everywhere they look. They can shoot weddings, portraits, and commercial work for businesses. Why, the sky's the limit, right? It's easy to convince oneself of the genius of one's own ideas and get carried away when thinking of photographic business ideas. Brainstorming is central to new business development, but at some point it is necessary to fine tune the business model and weed out the impractical ideas.

Many people have poor business sense. They may have overconfidence in their abilities to handle an assignment and overestimate their business acumen while failing to understand their target market. The world is not going to come looking for you just because you put up a website, pass out a few business cards, and tell a few friends about your new business. Instead, you need to carefully plan your business launch. Avoid spending money on things that you don't need. Develop a great marketing strategy. Develop expertise in a specific niche. Then you are on the way to setting yourself up for success.

Your clients are not paying you to learn on the job. You are expected to arrive at an assignment with everything you need to accomplish the mission at hand, take control of the photographic aspects of the job, and bring the assignment to a successful close by delivering what has been promised to your client. Everything that can be attributed to "acts of God" should be accounted for in your contract. There can be no excuses and no blaming others.

Blowing one important assignment that cannot be repeated, and as a consequence having to deal with an extremely unhappy customer, is often sufficient to put an end to the dream. Many photography entrepreneurs stop photographing altogether when a failure makes them realize that the business is not quite as glamorous as they had imagined.

Photography looks easy, and it can be if you spend time mastering the needed skills and developing your portfolio. Get out and meet the people who can help you develop your business. Network with those who can connect you to clients. Practice the type of photography that you intend to market, and then work on effectively marketing your skills.

Competition can be fierce in your chosen photographic specialty. There is so much competition that some are happy just to receive recognition. News organizations have been taking advantage of this by firing their photography staff and publishing images from so called "citizen journalists", journalistic integrity be damned.

Photographers seeking recognition from others can take charge of promoting their business by facilitating events that draw attention to their capabilities. Successful artists put as much creativity into self-marketing as they do into their photographic work. Start connecting with those who are in your target market or who can connect you to the gatekeepers that provide access to those markets.

Although there are many who spend too little time on developing their craft, there are many artists who are perfectionists to the point of paralysis. They can't finish any project they are working on because there is always something that can be improved. In reality, there must be a point at which the work is considered excellent, even if not perfect. This will become a major stumbling block to the commercial or editorial photographer who must meet a deadline.

As an experiment, create a concept for a project and shoot it just as you would on assignment. Put hard schedules and deadlines in place. Describe the deliverable in detail. Then shoot the assignment to completion. Can you produce an image that meets the requirements by the stated deadline? Analyze how you might improve the planning, the shooting, and the post-production to improve your quality or delivery time. Small wins are psychological boosts and build confidence. Practice isn't just about technique, but ability to deliver quality on a tight deadline.

Photographers' desire to be noticed and inaccurate assessment of the value of their work can make them easily exploited. There are a number of scams commonly perpetrated on creatives. A commonly encountered ruse is the promise of more work in the future in exchange for a discount on the project currently being bid. "Yes, your work is definitely worth $1000, but if you do this job for $100 we'll be able to get a lot of business and then we'll be able to pay you $1000 on the next assignments." Of course those $1000 jobs never come because they just move on to the next sucker with the same pitch. Be aware of such scams, but also educate yourself regarding the standard procedures for bidding projects, negotiating contracts, and managing accounts receivables.

Another common ploy is to either fail to pay or else pay very well past the due date of an invoice. Often a failure to pay is accompanied by a complaint regarding the quality of what was provided, or some other excuse. Late payments are often blamed on third parties, or the economy, or the government, or by some department in the company with which you're dealing. Photographers can also be scammed during the sales process by being pressured to reduce bids during price negotiations - "Joe down the street said he would do it for half your price. If you can't meet that price then we might have to use Joe", often under some kind of time duress such as an impending assignment -"We'll sign the contract after the shoot since the CEO is in the Bahamas till next week and we have to get this done this week." Never mind that the CEO can fax the contract. Another thing to be watchful for are last minute changes to requirements that were not in the original requirements specification - "We had to add three bikinis to the product shoot for this catalog." Changes are fine so long as the contract is updated to reflect them and they don't make the schedule unmanageable. Sometimes simple changes aren't so simple.

Not knowing what really goes on with many of these clients, naive business people may be resistant to "rocking the boat" for fear they will be "blacklisted". The reality of course is that most everyone else in the industry already knows the type of client they are and knows not to deal with them. You just haven't gotten the word yet. Even after conceding to some of these clients, giving up rights, working more hours than contracted to deliver more than was originally specified, this type of client might still refuse to pay the bill and further, threaten suit if you do not give your images away for free as a concession for some fabricated slight. A major clue that you are dealing with this type of client is their bragging about a prior lawsuit. It might seem odd to consider the idea of refusing business, however your time is your most important asset which you should dedicate only to those customers with whom you can develop a positive and professional relationship.

You Can't Have It

One thing you need to learn quickly is how to say No. A great salesman once told me about his favorite closing techniques. One of these was "You can't have it." You see, people seem to develop an overwhelming desire to acquire that which they can't have. "You can't have it" is a double edged sword. It can be used to motivate a client to action. But it can inadvertently be invoked in the way you decline an assignment from someone with whom you do not care to do business. We will delve into the sales process later so we won't address the use of this message as a closing technique here, however it is important to learn how to say No without invoking or stoking the need by the client. The message should be how much you want to help but can't see any way to do so, and things are totally out of your control. Specifics are not important and are better left out. Don't provide an avenue to circumvent No.

There are a number of lessons to be learned and a few hard and fast rules to follow if you intend to be successful in this business. Let's call these the Ten Commandments of Photography Business Success.

1. Never start work without a signed contract.

2. Always register the copyright on your images.

3. Always make the rights to use your images contingent on full payment.

4. Never permit a client to change requirements without signing a modification to the original contract which specifies the exact change and terms.

5. Always practice your craft and become proficient in any niche which you intend to market.

6. Never buy equipment for which you don't have a specific need, or for which rental is a viable option.

7. Develop a marketing plan for each niche market you intend to pursue and execute that plan.

8. Free is not a business model. Learn to say "No" to the client who asks you lower your price or give things away for free to "prove" something or for a promise of future business.

9. Don't try to be all things to all people. Choose at least one niche and become an expert in that area.

10.   Have fun with it. Life is too short to waste doing things that you don't enjoy.

If after reading this chapter you are still intent on pursuing photography as a career then read on. In the following chapters we will explore how to put these 10 rules into play. Each chapter has an assignment at the end. The purpose of the assignment is twofold. First, it helps to think about what you have read and put some of the ideas into action in your own life so that the book becomes less theoretical and more practical. Second, we may explore ideas which we will apply in following chapters and the assignment will assist you in getting up to speed with those ideas once they are presented. Let's get started!

Assignment

1. List the three types of photography you would like to do on a professional basis more than any others.

2. For each type of photography listed in #1, name three things about that type of photography that most appeals to you.

3. For each type of photography listed in #1, write your quick assessment of the market for that type of photography in your locale. For example, for "fashion photography", what are the market opportunities for fashion photography in your area? It's OK if there appears on the surface to be no local market, but the answer drives some choices you have to make in order to pursue it.

4. Create a detailed estimate of your annual living expenses, not including money spent on photography equipment. Include everything you and your family needs including food, shelter, utilities, transportation, medical expenses, insurance, etc.

2. Employee or Entrepreneur?

I often see questions asking how one might find a job as a photographer. If you are considering looking for a job working for another photographer or for an institution that employs photographers then you should analyze the implications of your decision compared to working for yourself. Determine whether it is the correct course of action for your situation. In some cases it would make more sense to start out on your own and in others it makes sense to start out working as an employee prior to a transition to your own business. There are also some photographic positions that tend to only exist in an institutional setting, such as medical photography. You should examine the competitive situation for both the employment and entrepreneurial alternatives, responsibilities and time requirements, potential for career growth, ability to access specific types of clients, and your ability to seek out new business and negotiate contracts. You also need to have a realistic assessment of the security or *perceived* security of a job versus the freedom and risk associated with running one's own business.

Some photography positions have absolute requirements in terms of education. For instance, medical photographer positions are usually only filled by those with a degree in medical photography. Photography teaching positions at the college level are usually filled by those with a Masters of Fine Art. In both cases it is unusual to see those with a degree in a different field getting hired for those positions.

Educational Considerations

Education is an important aspect of any photographer's career, whether as an employee or as a business owner. There are many educational opportunities of which one might take advantage in order to become successful. College and community college courses are usually accessible in nearly every locale. Community college courses can be very reasonable cost-wise and provide an opportunity to access equipment and software. This alone may be worth the tuition. Another approach to education that many photographers choose is attending professional workshops. These may range from local one or two day events to classes lasting a week or longer. Maine Media College and Workshops (formerly Maine Photographic Workshops) offer an incredible array of high quality instruction covering many topics of photography. The Professional Photographers Association offers workshops covering various aspects portrait photography business and technique. The American Society of Media Photographers (ASMP) offers both regional workshops and education tracks at its annual conference. Professional organizations often have a membership level for those starting out that provides access to mentoring programs. There are also specialist workshops for those that have a specific niche in mind such as headshot photography.

Competitive Landscape

There is no denying there is tremendous competition for the available photography jobs, even amongst highly skilled photographers. This is true across all genres. This has a direct effect on salaries for these jobs. Therefore, unless one has an extremely rare skill or combination of skills, it is quite likely that you may not be able to survive on the salary you calculated as your basic requirement in the first homework assignment. On the other hand, entrepreneurs must also keep the cash flowing, although the portion of the cash flowing to the entrepreneur photographer is likely to be much higher than that flowing to the employee photographer. In any case, there is no job security. You are only as good as your last assignment. If you are an entrepreneur you must keep marketing amongst constant pricing pressure from low ball competition and rights grabs by customers.

Entrepreneurship

There are great risks, responsibilities, and advantages to owning and running a business. Business owners must cover all of the expenses associated with running the business such as taxes, payroll, rent, insurance, equipment purchase and maintenance, and expendables. This requires keeping expenses at a manageable level. Inconsistent cash flow can be a problem. On the front end you must generate sales, but on the back end when customers are slow to pay you must act as the debt collector. In an ideal world one might institute a business model that prevents debts from occurring, but this is often impossible for some types of photography business.

The freedom of owning your business means that you get to set your own hours and you can run the business the way you think it should be run. You don't have to report to a boss for whom ethics is negotiable. You also have the freedom to fire clients who are not a good fit for your business.

Running a business requires discipline, persistence, tenacity, and integrity. Discipline means doing things the right way and not putting them off "until you have time". You soon learn that you have to make time. It means not taking shortcuts. Persistence means that you keep plugging away at your goal until it is achieved. Tenacity means you don't let adversity stop you from achieving your goals. Integrity means you do right by not cheating your customers or your employees, and by being truthful and fair in all of your dealings.

On occasion you must fire a bad customer. This might be one who abuses one of your employees, tries to cheat you, or has unreasonable expectations and demands on your time. Don't hesitate to let a bad customer go. You can do it without burning bridges or causing hard feelings. You can simply become "too busy" to take another assignment from that client. The bottom line is that you must stand up for yourself and for your principles. On the other hand, don't fall into the trap of becoming annoyed by a customer's needs. If your customer needs a favor like moving a delivery date up a bit, try to accommodate that request if it's in your power to do so. Build good will with your good customers.

Employment

When you choose to work for another company or institution you are in effect leaving the running of the business to the employer. They have the final say on decisions which may be different from how you would do things. Your job is to facilitate the decision to the best of your ability. With cell phones and email it is often less possible today to separate work and private life, but for the most part you get to forget about work when you are not at work. Although you are often paid less than you might be when you own your own business, you may have benefits that supplement your salary such as health insurance, paid vacations, and medical time off. Don't underestimate the value of such benefits and take those into account when considering multiple job offers.

Finding A Job In Photography

People tend to follow the path of least resistance. This often applies to those seeking photography employment. There is a tendency to look for jobs locally, and usually in the most obvious places. Let's consider an alternative approach that might make more sense for you in the long term. Surely you have a preference for the type of photography that you would like to do. You should have listed three of them in the first homework assignment. You must know of some great photographers in those genres. If you don't then do some research. Consider pursuing employment with one of those great photographers, or else a well established name who does similar work, or who worked with that photographer. Find out everything you can about the photographer. Start a communication with him or her. Sometimes you have to be in the right place at the right time in order to be hired for a position. You might even consider moving to the same city and finding other photographic employment to tide you over until an opening is available. Consider working as a freelance assistant. This can provide exposure to a number of photographers and keep you abreast of industry gossip. You never know when an assistant currently working for the photographer decides it's time to break out on his own. Be persistent but don't be a pest.

Assignment

1. Name three employers in your area who might hire a photographer on a full time permanent basis. What type of photography would this entail? Would you see yourself doing that kind of photography?

2. Name three photographers whose work you greatly admire. Research and learn what you can about those photographers. Where do they live? Which galleries represent them? Who buys their work?

3. Name at least three consumers of photography that might support the types of photography business that you think could be successful in your area.

4. Would you be happier owning your own business or working for a company as an employee? Why?

3. Choose Your Genre

Most professional photographers who are just starting out have yet to develop a regular client base.
There is a tendency in such cases to attempt to be
all things to all people and go after any type of photography assignment in order to find work. Clients,
on the other hand, tend to look for a specialist who
can solve their specific problem, not a generalist who *might* have the skills to do so. As a result,
those attempts on the part of photographers to
shoot anything that comes along will tend to backfire
and result in either less business or the very lowest
paying assignments than might be had if the photographer exclusively pursued his specialty in the
first place. Photography is used for many purposes
and may be categorized into a number of different
genres such as Editorial, Commercial, Portraiture,
Fine Art, and Event photography. There are further
subdivisions within those categories which we shall
delve into in more detail. Your first step in pursuing
photography as a career or business is to determine
which genre appeals to you most and validate that
choice in terms of the potential market demand. It
will do you little good to choose a specialty for which
there is an insufficient market in the area where you
intend to sell your services. The first assignment had
you list some types of photography that you would

like to pursue and the reasons for doing so. Using those as your focus, you can determine which genre would be most appropriate. Sometimes you can find an approach that lets you pursue a genre in an un-conventional manner in a market which might other-wise be difficult to crack, or one in which competition is very intense. Sometimes you may be forced to create a market where none exists. This is the idea behind the development and pursuit of a niche prod-uct or service offering. You might recall seeing those photography studios in tourist traps where you could dress up in a costume and have your portrait made against a fake background. That niche wasn't really practical until the technology made it easy to deliver the product to the customers while they waited. It took someone with the foresight to imagine and ap-ply the technology to the concept in order to create that successful niche.

Let's look at some genres to get a better idea what might be involved as a professional focusing on one niche exclusively.

Editorial

Editorial photography is used to illustrate, docu-ment, and inform. It is the primary source of images used in news, fashion, illustration, and documentary photography, each of which may be specialties within the editorial genre. News photography or photojour-nalism is the portrayal of people and events, presumably in a truthful and unbiased context. Fashion photography is used to promote and illustrate the concepts of fashion designers and tends to bridge editorial and commercial advertising photography. Much of the editorial fashion photography appears in conjunction with the advertising of the same products and displayed alongside fashion articles in fashion magazines. Fashion magazines and fashion websites are a driving force behind fashion trends and are controlled by the advertising dollars on which the magazines and related media depend. Other magazines which have a focus on celebrities or which tend to drive trends, also depend on advertising dollars from those driving trends. Technology has the same characteristics as clothing, cars, and jewelry in the fashion sense, all of which can to be aggregated under the umbrella of "Lifestyle". A typical editorial spread might show Joe Celebrity dressed in his Armani suit, flanked by models in Dior dresses, getting out of his Ferrari to take a trip to Monaco in his Learjet. All of the featured brands might wind up in full page ads in the same magazine. Local advertising follows similar patterns. For instance, a local publication might feature local businesses in a weekly column. The featured business will then place an ad in the publication.

Book publishers use illustrative and documentary photography extensively. Publishers often make use of stock photography. In cases where the required images may be too specific or rare to be accessible in stock archives they must be created for the publication or their use negotiated from owners of specific non-stock images. For instance a publisher of bird books might want a photo of a particular bird engaged in a specific activity. Such a special requirement may be well out of bounds for a traditional stock image library whereas it might be readily available from a photographer who specializes in photographing that particular species of bird. It is therefore advisable for those that produce stock photography to keep higher value images out of the stock libraries in order to maximize the profit from one's image archive.

Commercial Specialties

Commercial photographers are essential to the economy and produce images used to sell products and services. Commercial photographs are used in advertising, product labels and documentation, promotion of vacation and hotel properties, annual reports, and many other purposes. Manufacturers may either keep photographic staff employed to produce product images or they may contract the work out to a specialist vendor. A manufacturer may need to produce many different products in order to keep one photographer busy full time. Some companies have an art department with the responsibility to produce product images in addition to other types of illustrations. In either case, and given the goal of most businesses to minimize expenses, the trend is toward the outsourcing of such image and graphics production. If the company is not sourcing photography through an advertising agency then you may have luck approaching the company directly. Otherwise it pays to develop relationships with advertising agencies.

Advertising

Nearly every advertisement uses photography in some way, whether still or motion. Motion based photography often includes still photography. Advertising photography helps sell products by associating the product with a desired outcome, need fulfillment, or other emotional tie. As noted in the editorial discussion, fashion editorial and advertising imagery commonly occur in the same publication. The advertising images have a different character than editorial. They may be used to create a tableau, or fantasy world in which the product is featured, whereas the editorial images illustrate the news associated with the product or its manufacturer. For instance a beauty product will be used with a beautiful person to show that the user will be beautiful when the product is used. Editorial coverage may show an actress arriving at an awards ceremony wearing a gown by one of the designers advertising in the magazine.

An advertisement might illustrate ease of use of a product, showing the product in a particular context or in use with other products. Success in advertising photography requires skill in the creative and effective use of lighting, ability to work with demanding clients, a natural rapport with models and other creatives, and a great sense of design and attention to detail.

Product

Product photography is used to provide images of products for catalogs and websites, images used on product labels, as well as on the boxes in which products are sold. Closely allied to advertising photography, product photographs must show the product in its best light. The same skill sets and ability to work with clients are essential for success as a product photographer. There are specialties within product photography such as 3-D photography which permits a customer to view the product from all sides on a website. Product photography is often studio based, and access to a well equipped studio is often a criterion for success in the field.

Lifestyle

Lifestyle photography is the portrayal of people in a setting that illustrates specific activities such as sailing, traveling, vacationing, and entertaining, often engaged with family or friends. It may have an editorial or advertising bias depending on the purpose to which the images are to be used. Those portrayed may be real people, often celebrities, or they may be models or actors used to promote products or services in more of an advertising vein. Lifestyle photography can also be non-commercial and portray active subjects in a manner they might prefer over traditional portraiture.

Travel

Travel photography is used to illustrate travel destinations and businesses that service travelers such as hotels, restaurants, and resorts. It may include lifestyle photography to show people having fun at the destination, and it often includes architectural imagery of hotels, hotel rooms, and restaurants. Therefore, in order to be a successful travel photographer one must enjoy and be capable of shooting in a range of genres, enjoy traveling, have a high tolerance for stress, and be able to work effectively with people of different cultures. Familiarity with one or more foreign languages is useful as well.

Annual Reports

Annual report photography is largely editorial in nature and is primarily used to support the description of activities of a company and to promote the company's vision. It helps the investor reading the report to have a better understanding of the company's objectives and activities. Annual report photography should therefore support the mission of the company by showing it in its best light. Annual report photographs are often impactful and positive in nature. To be a successful annual report photographer you should be able to put together creative ideas from mundane business environments, work quickly and accurately, and enjoy travel. Travel can involve journeys to desolate locations with little in the way of accommodations for travelers.

Food & Beverage

People love to eat and they love artistically prepared meals. Food and beverage photography is used to promote restaurants, illustrate menus and recipes, and provide images for food products and other uses. The photographer specializing in food photography must be able to work quickly, have excellent attention to detail, and must work well with other creatives such as food stylists and art directors. Food and beverage photography can be highly specialized.

Headshots

Actors, models, and business executives are often in need of a headshot to be used in their self-promotion. Producing great headshots requires a photographer who is able to put people at ease, generate a great rapport with subjects, and be able to capture that fleeting moment when the subject reveals his true self. Headshot photography is a sub-genre of portrait photography. In large urban areas there is such a constant demand for good headshot photography that one can keep busy doing headshots exclusively. In fact, one can specialize and only shoot a particular type of headshot such as models, actors, or executives.

Portraiture

As people have become less formal and as digital cameras have taken over the market, the demand for large formal portraits has been in decline for many years. This is fortunate for a portrait photographer seeking a new niche since it provides a chance to give this niche a rebirth of sorts. There are specialties within the portrait genre such as family, adult, children, senior, infant, pet, and business portraiture. Any of these can be made a specialty, and within the specialty it is possible to specialize even further such as with special processes and other products.

Some photographers specialize in children and some in adult portraiture. Adult portraiture can take many forms, but one unique approach is boudoir photography. With boudoir, your objective is to make your subject as attractive as possible. A photographer who can make any subject look good can be very successful in this area. Women are the primary customers for this type of photography and they present the final images to their spouse or boyfriend, however the LGBT community is a potentially lucrative market for this type of photography.

Portraiture has traditionally been divided between what may be generally categorized as formal or informal portraiture. Formal portraiture is often done in a studio or client's home. Careful attention is paid to coordinating clothing and appearance of each subject. Whereas with informal portraiture it may be common to shoot outdoors, perhaps with a lifestyle approach showing activities and interests of the subjects.

Senior portraits are often a combination of formal and informal portraits. The formal images get distributed to the parents and relatives, the informal amongst friends. In some cases the informal images might involve lifestyle or travel oriented images in which a senior or group of seniors travels to a destination for a weekend of fun and photographs.

When most people think of portraits they tend to think of children and infant portraits. Indeed, when there is a new addition to the family everyone wants a photo. With the recent failures of portrait studio chain stores there may be an opportunity to fill a niche that was once dominated by low priced competitors. To be successful with this type of photography you must be able to work well with children and have high stress tolerance.

Fine Art

Fine art photographers produce images that are displayed for decoration and in some cases sold to collectors and museums. They may be sold in a number of venues such as art fairs, galleries, furniture and home furnishing stores, interior designers, and via the Web. Many photographers produce images that are published in magazines, such as images of birds and other wildlife. However, it is often the case that such publication is for little or no money. The photographers use that exposure to help market their work that is sold in the aforementioned venues. Some of the most successful fine art photographers produce a large amount of work that is sold at art fairs.

Event Photography

It's funny how one of the highest risk areas for professional photographers is often the most likely one to attract a fledgling photographer. Weddings are difficult to photograph well and new photographers are very likely to make serious mistakes in shooting one. Yet wedding photography seems to be the one field that is most likely to attract the new photography entrepreneur. There are other events besides weddings that are less prone to error and are likely better candidates for beginners. Family reunions and parties are typically casual or informal events where coverage consists of simple group and table shots. Other social events such as bar mitzvahs and Quinceañeras have a risk profile similar to weddings. The images produced are typically keepsakes for the family. Those attending often see relatives and friends they rarely see or may never see again. Photographers often sell many photographic prints from these types of events, predominantly in smaller sizes. For a family reunion a large group photo is often requested and those might result in a large number of orders of a larger sized print. Larger prints are the norm when groups sizes get very large making it difficult to make out the people in the group in small images.

Choose One Specialty

You cannot be everything to everyone. Choose a single specialty on which to focus your efforts to become proficient and make sure that it is something that you would like to become great at over the long term. It's OK to do personal work in other genres, but don't mix the two professionally unless you are creating a new niche, or it is a field that necessarily requires skills in multiple genres such as travel photography. Sometimes a personal interest or hobby may drive your choice. For instance if you are a wine aficionado you might produce still life images focusing on wine and sell those into markets which use that type of imagery.

As we have seen, we can divide photography into a number of genres such as editorial, advertising, fine art, events, portraiture, and commercial. Within those divisions there are specialties. Don't be the person who tries to be a Jack of all trades. Master one genre or a specialty within a genre and you will be more likely to find success as a professional photographer. As you progress professionally you may find yourself pulled into other niches, however trying to master multiple areas of expertise at the start will dilute your focus and growth in any of them.

Assignment

1. Which genre of photography most appeals to you? Why?

2. If you chose one genre of photography to follow and an opportunity for an assignment in another genre was presented to you, what would you do? Why? Give an example.

3. Some genres of photography require you to work in solitude while others require interacting and managing people. Do you think your genre of interest is a practical choice for your personality type? Why or why not?

4. Specialize

Don't Be a Generalist

Those who are the most successful in a field tend to specialize in some area. In photography, generalists tend to be hired for low paying minor assignments and specialists are hired to tackle challenging work requiring specific expertise. Although specialists tend to charge more for their services, clients know that hiring an expert will save them money over paying someone to learn on the job at a lower rate. It just makes good business sense. For instance, an advertising agency needs a photographer to produce an image showing a client's brand of beer being poured into a cold frosty glass mug. If you were the art director who would you call? You find two local options. Joe does wedding, portrait, and commercial photography. Jim is a food photographer who specializes in beverage pours. If the art director were to call Joe he might say "Yeah I can shoot a beer being poured." But, really, who do you think is most likely to produce superior results? Who is the art director going to choose? It's not just the ability of the photographer to get that shot, but also his knowledge of ancillary requirements and his ability to make suggestions that the art director didn't consider in the original design discussion. These are things of which the generalist usually has no knowledge. For instance, the experienced photographer might know to have a few pounds of dry ice on hand to help keep the mugs cold and add some misty visual excitement to the shot.

As we have seen in the previous chapter there are many genres in photography from which to choose as the primary focus of your business. There is no shortage of competition in photography, so whichever genre you choose as your specialty you need to become extremely good at it in order to be successful. In addition you need to become good at marketing to buyers of that specialty. No matter how talented you may be, it is impossible to do everything at an expert level. Every specialist learns subtle elements of his craft, fine nuances in image making, and efficient workflows that save time.

Those who are most successful in their occupation tend to specialize and make a name for themselves within that specialty. Likewise, you are most likely to succeed when you specialize within a genre or within a sub-genre, and make a name for yourself within that one specialty. Oddly, once you become known for a particular specialty you are quite likely to get called for that specialty exclusively. It is a good idea to take this into account when making your choice of a specialty. It may become difficult to change specialties after that association is made since your name will be strongly linked to the previous specialty. This is a common problem for wedding photographers who try to break into advertising or commercial photography. A Web search turns up the photographer's name as a wedding photographer rather than a commercial or advertising photographer and thus the credibility in the new field is challenged by the old association. It doesn't matter if we know that wedding photographers have to be good at creating great images the first time, it is the customer perception that matters most, and an advertising agency buyer might have an unfavorable opinion of wedding photographers.

It is very common and very easy to get distracted from one's primary mission and begin trying to pursue other types of photography that might pay *something*, particularly when starting out and business is slow. Try a different approach. When business is slow, work on your portfolio and try to come up with a new approach that is better than anything that your competitors are producing. Can you produce stock imagery that these buyers might have some use for? Competition can be fierce, with very good photographers in nearly every niche. You must stand out. Ask yourself why should someone hire you over someone else when looking for a specific product or service? People hire those who demonstrate a specific capability and have experience fulfilling that need. Sometimes luck is involved and a person makes a name for himself in a specialty after being asked to do something for the first time. Such luck is rare. Similarly, a person may become known for something after being asked to do so as the result of an existing relationship. This is probably the most likely sequence of events for many photographers who became associated with a niche with little prior planning. Hopefully, you are not leaving your success up to luck. Think strategically and pursue your goal by focusing on your niche, honing your craft, and building relationships with those who influence decision makers for the types of projects that you want to pursue. Let's say that your niche is beverage photography and you have invented a technique that produces an extraordinary image. Order a batch of large color postcards with that image on front and a simple message like "We are cutting edge!" and your contact information on the back, along with a description of your niche. Send those to the buyers with whom you would most like to work.

Wedding photographers often make the mistake of trying to take on commercial assignments for which they are ill prepared. That's not to say there may not be the occasional exception in the successful crossing of genres. For instance an editorial photographer might excel at shooting weddings since both types of photography have similar requirements. This is probably one of the most logical career transitions. Likewise an experienced wedding photographer might make an easy transition to editorial photography. One reason these are logical transitions is the requirement that they think on their feet, find a great image with little time to prepare, and must produce results the first time, without fail. A studio photographer might have more time on his side and might make many images trying to nail that one superb image. There are few retakes in news, editorial, or wedding photography. Nevertheless, your time would generally be better spent becoming the best in one genre rather than becoming a mediocre player in multiple specialties.

Specializing Within A Genre

It is often not sufficient to merely specialize within a genre. There are talented competitors in every photographic specialty. For instance, if you look at the wedding photography specialty you will usually find a large number of wedding photographers serving your area. It's likely that most of them provide the same commodity wedding coverage. Likewise, you have in most markets several commercial photography generalists servicing that market who produce commodity commercial photography consisting of business portraits and product photography. You must differentiate yourself from these other players in some way. This is often done by choosing a sub-specialty. Your market determines the feasibility of a choice to some degree, as well as your ability to create interest in the niche you are trying to carve out from the existing offerings. It's entirely possible and even advisable to attempt to create a new niche in your market. For instance, many people have an appreciation for black and white film photography. If you live in a large metro area, or if you are willing to market to an area beyond your locale, it might be possible to carve out a niche as a wedding photographer who shoots black and white film. Traditional black and white prints on silver halide paper have both a visual appeal and longevity that makes this specialty marketable. It provides sufficient snob appeal to attract high budget clientele. Competition in such a niche is a risk that must be analyzed. A niche such as black and white film photography requires technical discipline for its successful execution. The likelihood of a competitor being able to succeed against a technically competent and creative photographer may tend to be much lower than other wedding photography sub-specialties. Ultimately you must perform your risk analysis and make your decision based on the outcome.

Editorial photography is another example where a sub-specialty makes sense. Within editorial photography is the sub-specialty of sports photography. You rarely see sports photographers who cover all sports. Many of the most successful sports photographers specialize in just one or very few sports. For instance, there are sports photographers who cover car racing events. They develop contacts within the sport and gain access that a generalist might never achieve. The specialization can become much finer. For instance, within racing there are very specific types of racing events such a Formula 1. Contacts and relationships may take a long time to develop and they rarely cross lines from one type of racing to another.

Any intersection of high public interest and photography is likely to result in competition. However we don't just quit and go home, we look for opportunity not being exploited by others. It's safe to say that once you have established a niche and become successful that others are going to try to mimic your success. The goal is to establish your dominance in the niche early on and establish the connections you need to stay successful. There is some marketing and schmoozing involved. For instance, if you have started shooting races and you get a great shot of one of the drivers you might make that driver a print and send it to him with a short note. Such simple actions are remembered. Some day when you need access to that driver for an interview or photo session that past favor might pay off.

The key in establishing a market presence is to productize a specialty within a genre. Here are a few of the many examples:

Commercial

Food

Beverage

Soda

Pours

Wine

Restaurant

Location

Menu items

Desserts

Portraits

B&W

Large Format

Wet Plate

Boudoir

For instance if you are a food photographer then you might prefer to shoot beverages. You might live in wine country or you might live in a city with several independent small breweries producing craft beers, so you might gravitate towards one of those as a specialty. Your market then is pretty well defined and you might have a small base of local clients who help you get started. As your skills increase and you become better known, others in need of the type of images that you produce will begin to seek you out when they have a specific need in your specialty.

Limiting your customer base may seem non-intuitive, particularly to those just starting out and looking to generate income as a photographer. It's true that only people looking for someone specializing in the genre or sub-genre are likely to hire you. That's exactly the reason why you specialize. People are busy and have little time to bring you up to speed on what they do or what they are looking for. In fact, many are looking to you, the expert, to tell them what they need to know and do. So, yes, you will miss out on business that is intended for specialists in other genres. That's the point. You want to be the "go-to guy/girl" for your specialty. The only way to achieve that goal is to establish yourself as that person by making a name for yourself in that specialty, not in something else that distracts you from your mission and confuses potential customers as to your skill set. Besides the fact that it distracts you from your goal, the other business may not pay well due to competitive pricing pressure.

Remember that you are being paid for your experience, expertise, and *efficiency*. If you are paid more but save your client days of production time then you are worth much more to the client than the "cheaper" option. As the expert you are unlikely to make the rookie mistakes that the non-expert in the field may tend to make. Something as deceptively simple as a bride and groom portrait is a great example. If the bride's dress is not properly arranged by the wedding photographer, the portrait will be an unrecoverable disaster. Newbies have no clue about this and will typically leave it up to an attendant to make some type of adjustment, but usually with insufficient attention to detail. Likewise, as a beer pour specialist you might know tricks of the trade to get a perfect photogenic head on the first pour, saving your client time and money in the process.

 Don't lose sight of your goal to become very well known for a single specialty that you can execute better than anyone else. It is easier to schedule long term business if you are in demand for your specialty. If you are constantly scratching for small jobs to cover the bills then you will be continuously looking for anything and will never be able to schedule time off. The specialties often occur in context. For instance, the wine as part of a dinner layout. Your specialty doesn't preclude you from shooting such a layout, in fact your expertise with wine may be the very thing that distinguishes the result from an approach your competition may use. Jumping genres is often a bad idea, but moving up or down in your hierarchy is often necessary.

Niches

 Let's explore niches in a little more detail. As it pertains to photography, we can define a niche as a specialty within a genre which requires special equipment and/or skills to execute with superior results. When we have referred to specialization we have really been starting to talk about niches. In one of our examples we examined the specialty of *Commercial:Food:Beverage:Pouring* in the food photography hierarchy. The person who specializes in this niche excels in procuring superb images of beverages being poured. This type of specialist is in demand for production of beverage images, such as for beer or liquor advertising, or in any food related usage for which a beverage pour is featured. Within portraiture we might see a niche of *Portraiture:General:B&W:Large Format Silver Print*. The person who specializes in this niche shoots portraits on large format film and produces black and white silver prints. This niche might be called upon from a small number of discerning consumers, as well as from advertisers and corporate executives. Don't underestimate the power of owning a niche.

Why use a niche? A niche permits you to become the sole provider or member of a very select group of providers for the specialty. This is especially true when you create a niche where none exists. A niche permits you to offer workshops dedicated to that niche, which is a very legitimate means of profiting from those who start to compete with you in a niche that you created or dominate. If you are a thought leader then you have double the opportunity to sell your specialty. On the front end you become the only or dominant player in your market. Then as interest builds and followers start trying to compete, you have the opportunity to raise your fees while generating workshop income from the followers. You are able to raise your fees because you are the well known expert in the technique, despite the existence of new competition.

Another reason to pursue a niche is that customers like having something exclusive to brag about, whether it's an incredible shot or being able to afford a celebrity photographer (you). It is easier to start a meme around a niche. A meme is an idea that spreads like a virus through a population. In terms of your niche, the meme is the idea that your niche is perceived as "cool" or something that only a few people have access to but everyone should want. For instance when a new product is released there is often a lot of buzz on social media about the product's cool features and how few of the product will be available. This might lead to long lines at stores selling the product on the first day of release. These customers have been infected with the meme that they must own the product and will endure unpleasant conditions to acquire the item, be it an iPhone or other product.

It is very easy for people to decide they have to have something once they have learned about it and there is excitement about it amongst their friends and colleagues. Interestingly, it is often easier to create a need for something than it is to mitigate that perceived need. In many instances memes result in free advertising. As excitement builds it becomes easier to get media attention. Free PR is often some of the best advertising. Looking at wedding photography again in terms of memetics (the study of memes), you don't see many stories about wedding photographers other than negative stories when a disaster occurs, but you might see one about the wet plate wedding photographer who shoots weddings using equipment more common in the 1800s. It piques readers' interest and is one of those things that would prompt a wealthy person to spring for a wet plate photograph, perhaps as a gift to his daughter on the day of her wedding.

To create and occupy your niche there must be a market for the product or service you intend to sell, even if you have to create the market from scratch. There must ultimately be sufficient buyers for what you are selling for you to remain in business. Suppose you decide to create a niche as a photographer of food for menus for new restaurants. A market has an *area* and a *density*, the number of potential customers per area. For instance a market area might be defined as the Chicago metro area and the market density the number of new restaurants that open in Chicago each year. Your *penetration* in that market might be quantified as the yield in terms of business acquired, on average, from the new restaurants in your market area. The area might impact your throughput, or number of assignments that you can complete. For instance you may have to travel to meet new clients and to shoot the food at the restaurants. The larger the area the greater potential travel time that may be required. In some cases you can group client meetings, but grouping may not be possible on shooting days. For very large market areas travel might even take a half-day to full day.

Don't make the mistake of trying to create a niche for a market which cannot exist. For instance, if the market you can service has only a couple of restaurants then you would have little success selling menu photography services. There may well be a niche for the traveling menu photographer who visits a city for a few days to shoot and then moves on to the next city. This might be a viable way to market where a local business might not be practical.

Before you put a lot of effort into creating the niche, consider a few basic questions. Who is the buyer for the product or service? Where is the subject or things being photographed? Why will (or should) they be interested in what you have to offer? What differentiates you from the competition? What can you do or learn to do that will be difficult for your competition to replicate? What does the competition offer that you don't or can't offer? Can you use that to your advantage? For instance, in a discussion with your client, she mentions competitor X. You can counter by saying that competitor X specializes in Y, not what you specialize in. Furthermore, consider whether you and others can collaborate by offering your own specialties. For instance, the photographer whose niche is portraits of large groups using a banquet camera might collaborate with another photographer who specializes in event coverage.

Be realistic in choosing your specialty and establishing a niche. Don't quit your day job just yet. It is easy to convince yourself that an untapped market exists. It might or it might not. If it does, then there is still a question whether you can access that market and most importantly, close sales. Therefore, don't expend much time and money pursuing such a market until you can prove to yourself that it is viable. Ease into it. For instance, someone might ease into large format portrait photography by purchasing a Crown Graphic or similar inexpensive large format camera and using that to create a portfolio with which to procure initial work. Any further equipment expenditures would be put on hold pending validation of the business idea. If the idea doesn't pan out then the camera can be sold for approximately the used purchase price.

Assignment

1. Create a hierarchy list for sub-genres within the genre of photography you would like to work.

2. Define some niches that you might want to dominate within your sub-genre.

3. Assess the potential market for these niches.

4. How would you market to these niches and make a name for yourself?

6. Art Photography

There are a number of paths one might take in creating and marketing art photography. We will examine a few of these approaches and some market opportunities. This can't be an exhaustive list and I won't try to make it one. There is little point in trying to define art or art photography as this is best left to the academics, but it is useful to examine the available markets for a number of different approaches to selling art photography in order to demonstrate the potential as well as the need to be efficient with respect to selling your work. Some areas we'll look at include Landscape and Nature, Wildlife and Birds, Abstract, Tableau and Construction, Street, Still Life, and Floral photography. Next we will examine some niches in the production and sales of art photography. For our purposes we'll simply say that art photography refers to photographic images that are used for decorative, experimental, or non-utilitarian purposes. You are welcome to create your own definition. Although documentary and editorial photography is often seen in art museums, we don't include such here even though there is some obvious crossover. Such exhibits are often part of retrospectives of photographers. There is no requirement for other genres to be artistic in the sense that they appeal to common purveyors of art images (galleries and museums) but it is often the case. In fact, editorial and documentary photography might often be seen as more artistic than that which is produced as art in a more experimental vein. Therefore, I wouldn't get too worked up over the classifications, but do realize that some art you create will not be considered appropriate for some products and venues. You might find that your work is of interest to a museum but only be able to sell it to a handful of collectors. On the other hand, if you produce work that is appealing to hotel and corporate buyers you may find a steady market yet be unable to show the work in art galleries and museums due to its characterization as decorative art. People like to pigeonhole and classify people and it is easy to be cast as someone you are not and have no desire to be. Carefully consider where you show your work if you have specific long term objectives for a particular market or what you want associated with your name. Only show your work where doing so will help you achieve your long term goal.

Landscape and Nature Photography

Landscape and Nature Photography is what most people naturally think of when they think of art photography. Many are reminded of the grand and eloquent masterpieces of Ansel Adams and his contemporaries. Prior to his work nature photography often had a more expressionist quality that tended to mimic in some ways the work of painters. Landscape and nature photography finds many outlets. It may be found in museums and galleries but the majority is used for products such as note cards and calendars, and for decorative prints in homes, hotels, and office spaces. There is much landscape photography on the market and there is much competition on stock photo sites amongst such images, therefore it is difficult to generate a sizable income stream from stock images. Similarly it would be difficult to achieve a decent income stream by marketing images to producers of card and notebook products or other mass market goods. A better approach might be to become a competitor to the producers of these products by creating and selling your own products. Although there are outlets that allow you to sell products of your design for which they serve as the manufacturing and distribution mechanism, the profit margin might be significantly lower than if you own the means of production, create everything yourself, and handle your own sales and marketing. For example, you might create a line of note cards that you print, package, and sell at craft fairs or sell to gift shops. Nearly every industry has a trade show at which you can market to a large audience of buyers, so there is no need to think your market should be limited to a few local gift shops. Craft and art fairs are an excellent venue for selling landscape and nature photography. Success requires investment in equipment needed for displaying your work such as a tent and hanging system, bins for holding loose prints, and the ability to produce work that appeals to those who decide which artists are allowed to show work at the event. You must also be good at interacting with prospective customers and closing sales. Buyers of such work often want an easy solution to a decorative problem. Strategies such as providing free shipping of a framed piece to a buyer may provide that added motivation that results in a sale.

Every business needs art to display on their walls in order to provide a pleasing work environment. Professionals such as doctors, lawyers, and dentists usually have several works of art on display. Corporations and hotels may use large quantities of art. Some corporations are proud of the art they display and look for exclusive and unique pieces, whereas others take a more interior design oriented approach and look for art that complements the rest of the decor. Hotels often have a theme to which they match the art they display. The art used and displayed may not be limited to landscape and nature photography, but if you start paying attention to what is often on display you may notice there is a strong landscape and nature photography influence in many instances. Where landscape and nature is not a theme, strong graphic design often is, and thus provides a separate niche market for art photographers who produce images of a more abstract nature.

Corporations often buy art through an agent, so a good way to market to these organizations is through art buyers and interior design consultants. Make connections with as many interior design people you can and ask them where they go to find photographic art. Show your work and try to get connections to these gatekeepers. Again, trade shows can be a good place to market your work. Although art galleries are where most people think they need to market their work, the reality is that galleries move a small amount of work and are very selective about the work they show, making it extremely difficult to use galleries for a significant amount of sales. Likewise, museums may occasionally purchase works, or may receive art as gifts from supporters, but acquisitions are few and far between for the most part and often target well known artists. Museums are probably more active in borrowing collections from other museums.

Today landscape photography has a wide interpretation and may include urban landscapes, small scale landscapes including macro photography, or similar conceptual approaches in addition to more traditional scenic landscape photography. Develop a marketing strategy for each body of work in order to target buyers for whom the new work would appeal. For example a series of urban views of transit cars traveling in the city might be marketable in many venues as well as something that might appeal to a local history museum, particularly when the images reflect a time long past. This is an important point to remember. The images that you make today may not have value or be of interest to anyone until many years later. For instance a pub may open and seek historical photographs of the area to display to enhance its ambience. This makes both cataloging and copyrighting your images extremely important. You may need to be able to quickly find photographs that you made in years past in order to make a presentation and complete a sale. But you may also need to collect for a copyright infringement in the case your previously published work is stolen. The potential value of your photographic archive also means that you must have a dependable backup and archiving strategy. The strategy must be followed in order to protect your work from loss.

Wildlife and Birds

 Animal photographs have universal appeal. They have a high consumption rate by magazines, calendar producers, and websites, but there are also many photographers creating wildlife and bird photographs of very high quality who are competing with each other for sales in these markets. In fact, the most successful wildlife photographers are those who sell photography tours to supplement their income from the small number of photographs that they sell to magazines, particularly considering the low fees often paid by publishers. This is simple supply and demand. There are many images from which a publisher can choose so they have become brazen both in what they are willing to pay as well as the rights that they expect to receive for works they publish. Like landscape photography your best bet for selling your images may be to self-publish your work as books, note cards, and fine art prints sold through arts and crafts shows and to market your large images to buyers using images to decorate offices, hospitals, and hotels. Wildlife and bird images are often used in business settings where children are involved such as pediatric doctor offices, children's hospitals, nurseries and play schools, toy stores, and the like. A design consultant with a medical specialty might provide an excellent outlet for such images. Images capable of extreme enlargement, such as large format and panoramas, are particularly suited for such environments as they can easily be made into wall murals.

Wildlife photography often requires a significant investment in long and fast lenses in order to produce superior work. The long focal length allows you to fill the frame with your subject, making it possible to produce very large images when desired. The fast lens permits use of fast shutter speeds in low light conditions and more importantly, permits isolating the subject from the background.

Most stock photography agencies are so overwhelmed by wildlife images that you may have difficulty having any accepted. If they are accepted there is so much competition for attention in stock photo archives you are unlikely to see much income from sales, barring any truly unusual photographs such as an animal making a funny face, the type of thing that might appeal to an advertiser looking for an attention grabbing image. Truly rare images such as difficult to photograph bird behavior are best kept out of stock libraries and only made available to those willing to pay a premium for such images.

Abstract

 Abstract is a very interesting approach to art photography that has appeal to the entire spectrum of art buyers including collectors, corporations, hotels, museums and galleries, as well as consumers of goods on which artistic images might be printed such as note cards, calendars, and the like. A simple definition of abstract photography is that which combines elements of form and design in a creative way. Often you cannot determine the scale or source of the composition, or it may be an interesting view of something obvious. Strong contrast of light and dark, or of color, often contributes to such compositions. Abstract images in many cases represent pure forms, interesting plays of light and shadow, unusual patterns in everyday things, and similar visual elements that cause an inquisitive person to peer in and try to decipher the context and meaning of the image. One might argue that abstract is the purest form of photography and that might be a reason it has such universal appeal.

In addition to the wide appeal held by abstract photography it is possible to produce marketable work with minimal equipment. In fact, at a recent juried show I saw three works by a photographer that were taken with a toy plastic camera. They were abstracts of urban landscape elements, nicely framed and mounted. All three sold the day the show opened and were among only a handful of images marked as sold during the opening reception. It just goes to show that you do not need thousands of dollars worth of expensive gear to produce work that will sell.

Tableau and Construction

Tableau and construction photography, like abstract photography, tends to have wide appeal to a range of buyers, although it does tend in most cases to be somewhat less marketable than pure abstract photography. It does of course depend on the visual elements in the images, whereas abstract photography tends to be less dependent on the constituent visual elements. A tableau is a combination of elements that together form a visual story or juxtaposition. It might be something like a room with interesting elements, or people interacting in some way. It can be on a small or grand scale, with many actors or only one. It is always staged rather than a chance composition as street photography often portrays. In some cases the visual elements are combined using software as in a photo montage. Each element might be photographed separately, perhaps using green screen techniques. These elements would then be brought together layer by layer in photo editing software.

Construction photography is similar to tableau photography. In this context we do not mean photographs of construction sites. Visual elements are combined to create an interesting scene. In this case the visual elements typically do not involve people. More often they are combinations of three dimensional objects combined in an interesting way and photographed. For instance, sheets of paper might be cut into shapes and folded or rolled that when combined produce an interesting image, perhaps accentuated with interesting lighting effects. Construction photography tends to be content neutral like abstract photography, thus making it have wide appeal. This type of photography works well in corporate and hotel environments and could easily support a requirement for large images. For example, a boutique hotel might have a requirement for a large image for its lobby. One marketing approach would be to create a series and sell both the large lobby image as well as smaller supporting images from the series to place throughout the rest of the hotel such as in elevator lobbies and hallways.

Of the more sought after images of interest to collectors currently, tableau photography tends to rank fairly high amongst those procuring work of new photographers. It remains to be seen whether the trend continues or if more traditional stalwarts such as abstract photography again take the lead.

Street Photography

Street photography holds appeal for many photographers, most of whom are familiar with the classic street images of Henri Cartier Bresson. Although street photography is a popular photographic pursuit it has low marketability due to the limited number of appropriate venues for its display. Hence it is often found in galleries and private collections, but rarely used in more commercial contexts. If you are an avid street photographer your best route to marketing your work might be direct sales of your prints and books from your own website. The best street photography often features interesting juxtapositions of visual elements and color. A common theme is some type of visual pun, a play of some element such as a sign against a person doing something suggestive or in contrast to the message on the sign.

Still Life and Floral Photography

Still life and floral photography appeal to a wide range of art buyers and can find a market in nearly every segment similarly to abstract photographs.

A still life is a composition of objects which may or may not have something in common, but have a pleasing relationship in the context of the image. An example where things have something in common is the classic shot of a bottle of wine, a wedge or round of cheese, bread a on cutting board, a cluster of grapes, etc. An example where things don't particularly have anything in common might be something like a book, ball of twine, knife, and an old tennis shoe. Often the items are shot against a hand painted studio backdrop or other neutral context. These compositions have wide appeal. In some cases they make excellent art to display in a particular setting, such as a still life of wine bottles in a restaurant or wine merchant.

Floral photography is a type of still life photography featuring plants and flowers. The images might feature an entire flower or close-ups of components of flowers. In fact, it is often the case that the visual elements of an abstract image originate from features of plants and flowers. Some photographers specialize in abstracting elements of flowers.

Portraiture

In addition to portraiture being a genre in itself for the purpose of producing marketable work, portraiture is widely created as art. Again, we don't need to get too worked up over classifications and definitions since we are primarily looking at ideas for marketing photography. Portraits and figure studies have been made for as long as people have been photographing. Couple your passion for portraiture with a unique vision, special processes, and interesting subjects. You should find a wide market for your work amongst art buyers and the subjects of your images. If you research art auctions you will find that portraits of historical figures tend to sell well, therefore think of this type of photography as having both short term and long term value. Producing a set of prints and holding them for a period of time may well be a worthwhile investment of your time and materials, particularly if you cultivate relationships with up and coming artists and politicians, for whom the interest in historical images is strongest.

Portraiture can also be a tremendous opportunity for stock image sales. Whereas the market is fairly saturated with wildlife and nature stock photography, buyers are always looking for fresh images of people for ad campaigns. As was recently pointed out by a news commentator, an image used in a political ad meant to portray supporters was also used for selling other products. Art portraiture sought by collectors differs from portraiture used for stock imagery. The deadpan poses and context in which much of the collectible art world tends to pursue is much different from the types of images used in advertising, such as the happy family waving from the wooden bridge alluded to earlier by the news commentator.

Niches In Art Photography

There are many niches in which one might specialize with respect to art photography. Beginning with the type of equipment used, the process and techniques used in creation of the prints, as well as display options. If one is photographing with the intent of selling through galleries there might be an advantage to shooting film rather than digital, with black and white often preferred over color, although this may be changing as galleries are seeing that prints from inks may tend to have a much longer life than historic analog color images. The camera one uses doesn't tend to matter, although from a practical standpoint if one is making photographs such as those of birds that require special equipment, then acquiring or renting the long lenses and other equipment would seem to be a requirement. However, as noted earlier, in some areas like abstract photography success is often achieved with something as simple as a cheap plastic camera.

The technology used in the production of prints that are sold is another factor. This is partially dictated by the final size you intend to produce. An alternative process such as platinum/palladium is certainly an excellent niche to be able to fill, but is not practical for production of very large prints, both from a cost and logistics standpoint. Very large silver prints are also challenging to produce. Silver prints have consistent demand from art buyers. Consider the tradeoffs involved when choosing a process. It is possible to maintain a niche that separates you from the rest, but you may prefer to use a friendlier process such as carbon ink sets in an inkjet printer if you need to print very large prints. Such a compromise would permit you to efficiently print very large prints yet be confident in the long term archival stability of the image. For smaller images there are several possible niches one might fill for the production of art photo-graphs. On the other hand if you are printing small prints in the 4x5 to 16x20 range, then there are a large number of alternative processes from which to choose. Each alternative process has its own char-acteristic look and skill set required to produce nice work on a consistent basis. Therefore, it takes time and commitment to master that technique. There is little point in producing work in a number of different processes. Experiment and find one that works best for you and your work. Stick with it until you can achieve consistent results that reflect your vision. Nearly any alternative process may be used so long as it produces long lasting images.

Finishing Fine Art Images

Finally, once you have created and printed your im-ages, you may want to package and present them to the buyer in a manner that reflects the same quality and attention to detail that you put into production of the images. If these are small prints to be sold at an art fair then hinge mounts in window mats is a common format that is inexpensive to produce, looks great, and is an archival best practice. You can extend your vision to the creation of custom frames that accentuate your work, thereby acting as an extension of the print. Some people might consider that approach a gimmick and others might be quite appreciative.

An exceptional display I saw recently featured a series of simple images printed on aluminum. The aluminum was mounted to a block of wood using tacks at the four corners. The wood was painted flat black. The artist did not share her process, but the effect looked somewhat like wet plate. The artist showed this work in a coffee shop in November, right before Christmas. The price was appealing and I'm sure she sold many of her works to be given as Christmas gifts.

Large prints present special display challenges. You must weigh the trade-off between archival and display features as well as cost. For instance some photographers face mount their work to acrylic. It is thus permanently affixed to the mounting system and is therefore subject to ruin if the substrate is damaged. The same is true for other permanent mounting solutions. Consider the archival stability of all components used in the process of mounting and display of your art.

Assignment

1. What type of art photography would you produce if you thought you had a market for your work?

2. How would you let others see your work?

3. What types of products would you produce? How would you package them?

4. How could you market your work to reach the largest number of buyers?

7. Commercial Photography

Commercial photography is a wide ranging genre with many specialties, each having unique requirements in terms of marketing and production. Therefore it is impossible to provide any sort of complete guide to commercial practice. Instead we provide here a brief overview of a number of specialties within commercial photography. If there is a particular area that attracts you then the next steps would be to do your homework by doing a critical analysis of the market in the area you wish to serve, competitive analysis of the other vendors in that market, develop your marketing strategy, and produce a portfolio of top-notch work that is superior to that of all of your competitors in your chosen niche.

Commercial photographers produce images used by businesses and other organizations. There are several major specialties within the genre such as Architectural, Food, Advertising, Real Estate, Corporate Events, Political Functions and Events, Aerial, Executive Headshots, and many others. There is of course crossover between these specialties, for instance advertising photography for food products might be thought of as a specialty within the advertising photography realm. An architectural photographer might provide aerial photographs of a site using a drone. Commercial photography can be a well paying occupation for the photographer who can consistently deliver high quality images, meet deadlines, and work effectively with clients. This is a people business. You must be able to develop connections in the sphere of businesses with whom you would like to work. One approach for this is to join organizations which support the types of businesses you would like to work with, either as a general member or supporting member. You needn't join as a supporting member right off the bat, verify that the membership will be worthwhile to your business first. Supporting members usually get a plug at meetings and a banner or other advertising at annual or other major events. That type of thing is negotiable, especially with smaller organizations. For instance, if your specialty is architectural photography there may be a local society of architects. Attend a meeting and let those in charge know who you are and that you are interested in learning more about the problems architects face in terms of photographic services and that you want to better understand their needs so you may be more effective as an architectural photographer. You in essence work your way into being an ally to those in the field. You should not be seen as a competitor in this type of scenario.

Architectural

Architectural photography is used for editorial purposes, documentation of architect designs, advertising, and sales presentations. Editorial use includes articles in architectural and consumer magazines, books, websites, and other uses. Each building and interior designed by an architect is typically documented by photographs. These are used by the architect to show prospective clients their past work. Hotels, housing and commercial developers, and apartment complexes all use architectural photography in advertising and promotional materials. In many cases you will document both the interior and exterior space.

Architectural photography requires a sense of perfection and extreme attention to detail. No detail is too small to leave unattended, including the color temperature of each light source. Where interiors reveal an exterior view, the exposures of both scenes must be perfect. This includes exterior views which include a view into the interior, such as to show the interior from outside at dusk. This tends to be a good use to which to put high dynamic range (HDR) photography. A good exercise would be to examine photographs in Architectural Digest, consider how you would replicate the shot, try to think of a similar property that you could shoot, and also look for imperfections in the images. Then photograph a similar scene and try to achieve superior results. It's not easy.

Editorial architectural photography is used to document architects' projects for various purposes. In magazines and other media the primary goal is to sell advertising, therefore the articles in the magazines are most often complimentary to the advertising content of the magazine. If the magazine article promotes an architect look for that architect's ad somewhere inside. A building requires a builder so there may be advertising by builders as well. The same is true for interior designers and decorators. Therefore, examine publications in toto. You may find there is a market not only for the images that accompany an article, but for the advertising as well. Advertising is sold by the column inch. Smaller companies may buy smaller ads. At about a quarter page the justification for photographs becomes strong. Contact advertisers who run ads that do not contain photographs and try to sell them on the idea of increasing the ad size a bit while including photographs. When reviewing the work of architectural photographers pay attention to the design elements and the manufacturers represented in each scene. Lighting, plumbing fixtures, and others may be candidates for images of a manufacturer's products in a well designed environment. How are those brought to light in the publication?

 An excellent market for your architectural photography services is the hotel industry. Competition is fierce in the hotel industry and hotels are frequently updating their properties in order to appeal to customers. Be proactive by getting out into the community and meeting the hotel owners or managers. Introduce yourself and tell them that you are an architectural photographer and would love to bid on their next project the next time they have a need. If there are deficiencies in the images shown on their web pages then use that as an opportunity to show them that you can help them improve their sales with better images. You don't need to ask them directly if they need photography but if they do they will probably say so unless they already have a vendor with whom they usually work. In some cases that vendor might be a wedding photographer who has connections with the catering department, so there may be room for improvement. Just be friendly and compliment them on something you like about their property. Always make a note of who you contacted and what occurred during the call. Often a manager will move on and you may need to develop a relationship with the new manager. In this case when you pay a visit you can mention the previous manager by name so there is some implied familiarity.

New housing projects are another source of business for architectural photographers. When a housing development is being marketed one or more homes will be decorated as a model home. Photographs of the models are used in advertising and for review at initial client consultations. A book with these photographs may be distributed to the sales staff and they often have more in the sales office. Your point of contact for this type of photography is someone like a director of sales at the company developing the property and any exclusive real estate agent who they use to market the property if this is not done in-house. Again, pay a visit and tell them you'd like to be considered for future work. They'll let you know if they need help right away.

New apartment complexes are similar to housing developments in their need for photographs. They have a similar process of using a model apartment to show potential customers what a decorated unit might look like. Photographs of decorated units are used in advertising for print and web media. Housing rental companies run the gamut from small outfits with a single building to large corporations holding hundreds of developments. You can target these companies with a glossy postcard with examples of your work on the glossy side and your short marketing message and contact information on the other. The images you select should be representative of the type of photography they would aspire to have in their advertising, ideally just a cut above what they currently have in their current advertising. This raises an important point, when you see bad photography think of it in terms of a potential client. How can you help that client? Why don't you let them know?

Another potentially lucrative market for architectural photography is the high end real estate market. High end properties can be difficult to sell, so compelling images that make potential customers want to see the property are an absolute must. In addition to stunning images it is common to also produce 360 degree panoramic images that place the viewer in the various rooms of the home. To build this type of business, develop a portfolio of any high end property you can gain access to and approach real estate agents that specialize in the high end market.

Food & Beverage

Food photography is a fun and diverse specialty within commercial photography. Food photographers are needed to shoot food for restaurants, food products, editorial, beverage manufacturers, grocery chains, and for numerous sub-specialties such as vintners. The largest segment of food photography is probably images for advertising and product packaging.

Restaurants need images of their facilities, food, and employees for web, print, and television. Customers looking for a restaurant are attracted to clean facilities with the right ambience. Images of the food must be appealing. Restaurants range from the low end to very high end establishments. An assignment for a restaurant might consist of shots of their dishes as well as portraits of the chef and manager, and perhaps interiors and the exterior of the restaurant. One approach to marketing to new restaurants might be to create a restaurant startup package. When a business license is issued to a new restaurant you would send a promotional piece that offers three variations such as some number of dishes, portraits, interior and exterior shots for a set price. It's always a good idea to offer a range of choices. Some restaurants may have very simple menus while others have very extensive ones. You can partner with a print shop in your area who can provide printing services for signs and menus to offer even more extensive choices.

Grocery store chains often have specialty shops that make and sell food products such as baked goods. Create portfolio shots by shooting the food sold by some of these shops and used those in your marketing efforts to that type of customer. The photos might be used in signage, Web, and print advertising.

Large food manufacturers may have their own art staff in-house, however through cost cutting that can change and result in opportunities, therefore don't write off large companies as unapproachable for your food product photography services. This applies to beverage companies as well. It may be difficult to make inroads with large established ad agencies. Look for small boutique ad agencies that are just starting to land these large corporate accounts.

Large food companies are seeing more and more competition from the young upstart companies that are trying different approaches to disrupting the markets. Be on the lookout for new emerging brands with whom you can start building a relationship.

In some cases food photographs are used to promote the vendor selling the items rather than the items themselves. For instance, a high end wine store might purchase large still life images of a bottle of wine with a round of cheese and bread to provide an Old World ambience in the store. They might sell imported cheeses as well as wine and this type of image helps promote the sales of both products.

An interesting specialty within the area of food photography is liquid pours and splashes. This takes skill and special equipment to get pleasing results so a photographer who has the equipment and talent may be called upon by those needed this type of photography. Look in any magazine which has a high incidence of beverage ads and count the number of ads featuring the pouring or splash of liquid.

Advertising

Photography is used extensively in advertising. There are few goods advertised where photography does not play a role. Just a sample of advertising outside of the specialty of food includes clothing and accessories, hair products and makeup, sporting goods and outdoor products, furniture and products for the home, computers and consumer electronics, automobiles and accessories, and many more. Additionally, photography is widely used for the advertising of services. One can easily specialize in a single area and in fact it is common for a photographer to be associated with a particular specialty. For instance, someone may be known as the go-to person for extreme weather, outdoor and ski clothing photography. One reason would be they have the relationships with skiers and know the nomenclature used by skiers and therefore can be a more effective communicator. That same photographer may not be considered for other types of clothing photography for which other photographers may be better known.

Approach this type of photography like any other by devising a marketing plan and start working on your portfolio. Know your market and your competition. Look for weaknesses in your competition, or find where their strengths are and look at developing a niche that is outside their strong area of expertise. Since a photographer who is strong in a particular area is going to attract business from those who have a need for that specialty, develop your expertise in an area that is orthogonal to your competition. Alternatively, if you want to focus on an area in which there is strong competition, you need to develop a fresh approach that is very different from your competitors' offerings.

Fashion and clothing photography is used in catalog production, web sites, newspaper advertising, and television. Your pitch to these various consumers might vary according to the context in which the photos might be used. For instance, a pitch to a catalog company is consistency and ability to mix pieces from various manufactures to present a look that reflects the catalog company's style.

 If you would like to pursue the market for hair or makeup photography then you best partner with a makeup artist (MUA) or hair stylist who would likewise desire to serve the same market. Work together to create and photograph some very distinctive looks. The fashion shows in Milan and Paris tend to push the limits of style. Do the same with the work you create for your portfolio.

 Much product photography is essentially still-life photography. Although it is challenging to make an image of a product with perfect lighting, start to think outside the normal product photography box and try some more avant-garde presentations of mundane products. Think in terms of strong contrast. Think in terms of humor. Juxtapose elements of texture and context.

 Many commercial photographers are successful at creating and executing concepts for clients. These might be similar to large scale tableau projects one might create as an art photographer. They might convey a point in time of some complex scene or they might be smaller in scale. Conceptual photography, particularly that done on a large scale, requires extreme attention to detail and much planning and coordination. Every element must be accounted for and correct in the scene. Reshooting may be very difficult and expensive, so failure is not an option.

Photographers of very large productions are more on the level of directors, bringing all the elements together under with the help of a number of assistants, each responsible for some part of the whole. They must execute a concept on a grand scale, possibly employing hundreds of people. Aside from the technical requirements to get all parts of the scene in proper focus, nailing the exposure, and all the other basic requirements of a project, the director/photographer must be a master of coordination and command attention from those participating in the project.

Some commercial photographers specialize in shooting locations with extreme conditions such as snow and ice, desert, underwater, as well as in extreme sports scenarios such as skydiving, rock climbing, and sports aviation. These photographers capture action of products in use under the conditions in which they are expected to excel. Such photographers must not only be capable of producing excellent images but must have the physical stamina, endurance, and skills required to survive in these conditions.

Real Estate

Real estate photography would seem like a no-brainer in terms of people wanting good photographs to market their property, however the reality is that this is a difficult field in which to be successful. Real estate agents and brokers work on commission and they usually have so many properties they are trying to market it would not make economic sense to pay for photography for each one. The sellers tend to think that the agent is already charging them so much that they should be the ones footing the bill for any photographic coverage. For these reasons the primary market for real estate photography is for marketing very high end properties. What constitutes "high end" is dependent on the market you serve. In some cases it may mean a threshold of one million dollars, in others it might mean more or less. One way to pitch this to sellers and agents is that you only serve the top one percent of the market, and that such special properties certainly deserve the type of coverage you can provide. A prime candidate for this type of service is a property that has been on the market for a few months and which has little to no photography to show it off.

Corporate Functions and Events

One of the best commercial photography outlets for wedding photographers is corporate functions and events. In fact this type of photography is often requested by venues at which a wedding photographer is shooting. This is one reason it pays for wedding photographers to get to know the other vendors servicing the wedding industry. Companies often have trade shows and conferences as well as company functions and parties for which they need photographic coverage. The images might be used in internal publications, company blog, newsletters, and similar outlets. Members of the executive and sales teams often need headshots for the company website and other uses. This type of photography allows you to gain access to the decision makers in the company who may hire you for other work such as product photography. General business networking groups are good sources of introductions to those who may buy this type of service.

Political and Charitable Events

Political function and event photography is specialty in photography that gets little attention. These events are held by candidates and political organizations as well as political action groups and charities. Often there are important political figures or celebrities attending and this provides an opportunity for the organization or candidate to raise money. The organization may want to provide donors with a memento photograph of the donor with the celebrity. When you visit someone who has a photograph on the wall of them with a celebrity, it is very likely this was taken at just such an event. It is important to be able to keep track of who you are shooting in order to get the photographs distributed to the correct people. To market yourself in this specialty you need to develop a relationship with one or more political and charity fundraisers.

Headshots

There are two basic approaches to headshot photography. The high end of the specialty provides executive portraits to C-suite executives and celebrities. The low end of the market typically covers a steady flow of small business owners, tradesmen, beginning actors, real estate agents. The high end requires flawless execution and ability to make a compelling portrait with only the few minutes of the executive's time. There is no room for error and certainly none for fiddling with your equipment. You need to nail focus and exposure all the while producing top-notch work. Occasionally you will be asked to shoot a mass portrait session. You can usually do those in a rapid fire session. If you have an assistant getting a feed from your camera it is possible to have instantaneous quality control and easily perform a reshoot before the subject leaves.

Other types of headshots are those for actors and musicians. These are somewhere between the low and high end extremes and you usually have more time to work with the client, get some feedback, and produce a nice selection of work. In a large city a studio in a good location can generate steady work shooting headshots.

Commercial Niches

As we have seen, commercial photography is very specialized and tends to support those who establish themselves as the best in a well defined niche, the "go to guy" for that niche. The ideal situation is having expertise in a place in which it is difficult for others to compete, such as when you possess special equipment or knowledge of special equipment that permits you to do something others can't easily do. This might be something you build, for instance a special wet photography set that permits you to do splash photography well. Or perhaps acquire a high speed flash that lets you catch very fast action. The more highly defined your specialty, the more you limit your market, and thereby limit your sales. However, by becoming the high in demand expert you should be able to gain access to more lucrative and interesting assignments.

Marketing To Commercial Clients

It should go without saying that you will have a website that shows off your work. It should be very clean and modern looking and should work equally well on browsers on phones, iPads, Android tablets, and laptop computers. It should load fast. It should contain only your best work and that work should reflect the types of assignments you are interested in shooting. If you haven't done any of the type of assignments you wish to shoot then you need to shoot them on your own. Be the photographer you want your clients to see you as.

Next, sign up on one or two of the commercial photography portfolio sites. You might get an inquiry through this but it also serves to expand your Web presence beyond your website. Again, put up some of your best work. You don't need to go overboard, save some for your in-person consultations with clients.

Once you have these in place you can start contacting specific clients. One approach is with a 4 color postcard. On the glossy side print a few images that will appeal to your target customers. On the print side include a very short introduction and contact information. If you intend to follow up in a few days with a phone call, then go ahead and say you will be giving them a call to answer any questions they may have about your work. If you say you are going to call then do so. Postcard contacts like this are just like print ads. You need to keep them going out on a regular basis until they start to pay off. Sending one each quarter isn't a bad schedule.

Newsletters can be a very effective communication tool. If you provide a form on your website to allow customers to contact you, include a check box to give you permission to add them to your email list for the newsletter. Also include a signup form on your home page. Send your newsletter out on a regular basis such as monthly or quarterly. Use the opportunity to tell your prospective clients about the things you are up to, experiments you are doing or other projects, share ideas on how they can work more effectively with a photographer, update them on anything important they should be aware of pertaining to your work such as advances in technology or your capabilities, etc.

Trade shows and trade association events are a great way to make contacts. Add these contacts to your LinkedIn contacts list and your email or newsletter list provided they give you permission to do so. If you discuss something of mutual interest be sure to follow up later regarding that interest. Even if it's something more of a personal nature like a hobby you have in common, use it as an opportunity to better that relationship. Obviously, you would not go to a photography trade show to find potential clients. Go to the trade shows and association meetings that are attended by those in your target market. For instance, if you photograph food try to find a food industry association, such as the type attended by those looking for kitchen hardware, produce, etc. Speak to the vendors at these events since they too may be in need of images. This brings up a very important point. Companies do a lot of marketing at trade shows and they need both still and video content that grabs attention. Such imagery needs to be displayed large. This can result in sizable orders from customers seeking to make an impression at a show. Not all customers have the budget and some have no sense of aesthetics, but these folks are often rel-egated to the back rooms and poorly traveled areas of the convention center and may not be your target market. When you reach out to such customers a good question to ask might be "How do you want your trade show presence to be remembered?" Accompany that with a before and after photo or something of that nature to illustrate the difference.

Competitive Analysis

Competitive analysis is a process whereby one attempts to gain an understanding of the position of a potential competitor in the marketplace, their capabilities and skill level, and assess their success in the particular niche you are interested in pursuing. There are many methods one can employ to learn about competitors, and their use is contingent on the amount of detail you need to complete your assessment. Much can be learned by a comprehensive analysis of the information regarding the competitor which can be found on the Internet, starting with their website.

Website Analysis

One should make a qualitative assessment of the competitor's website. Does the competitor focus on a single niche or is the competitor a jack of all trades? Is the website well designed? Does the competitor provide easy to locate contact information and list the locale in which he practices? Does the competitor list prices and if so what are they? Does the website have a professional look and solid design? Does the website feature a portfolio? Does the portfolio feature work that is competitive in terms of your intended niche?

Is the competitor listed on other websites? Does the competitor have an agent? Is the agent local? Does the agent represent other talent in the same niche or is the representation broader in scope? Does the competitor write a blog? Does the competitor make comments on other website blogs or forums? Are articles and comments by the competitor more of interest to other photographers, or are they of interest to potential clients? Does the competitor use Twitter and Facebook? Does the competitor have any type of social media following? Does the following consist of potential customers or potential competitors? Does the competitor have listings on association or other agency websites where customers might look for a photographer? Make a qualitative assessment of the presence on those sites in terms of content, both images and text. Could you create a superior entry if you chose to advertise on the same site?

Another aspect of competitive analysis is evaluating the community presence of the competitor. Does the competitor have a physical location such as a storefront? How large is it? Where is it located? What overhead might the competitor have in order to keep the location? How many employees does the competitor have? What kind of vehicles do they drive? Is the competitor active in the community? In what way? Is the competitor active in charitable organizations? Business organizations? Organizations complementary to the niche you are pursuing? Can you increase your community presence respective to the competitor? How might you do this?

The amount of business analysis you might find worthwhile is dependent on the degree to which the competitor is working in the same niche versus the degree to which he is occupied in other areas. If his niche business is only a small part of the overall business then it's difficult to glean much information as to the amount of niche business he is doing. Some approaches that I have seen used include making purchases at two different times and seeing if invoice numbers indicate the number of transactions the business has conducted over the period; counting the number of people entering and leaving the premises; calling to schedule a shoot during a traditionally busy time in order determine how successful a competitor is in booking jobs during the busy times; calling for price information; participating in an in-person sales presentation to determine the effectiveness of the sales staff ; creating an RFQ for an assignment to see the type of bid the competitor might present to a customer. Again, such activity might require the assistance of actors and an off-site location at which to conduct meetings. Some of these approaches might be considered less than ethical, but you should consider the fact that your competitor might engage in the same type of analysis of your business. Therefore you might consider how to make your business less visible to those who might engage in similar activities.

There are sometimes clues to other business activities of a competitor to be gleaned from domain ownership analysis, however this is becoming more difficult with the introduction of anonymity features with domain registrars. Who owns the domain of the competitor's business? Does the same entity also own other domains? What business activities might be associated with these domains? Are they active domains with websites? Do any of these domains indicate a business presence in other niches, or are they totally separate industry domains? This can provide clues as to the seriousness of the owner in the niche you are pursuing, how thinly the competitor's resources might be spread in terms of dominating in that niche, etc.

A word about hacking. Hacking of computers, email, and networks is highly illegal and should never be considered as part of your competitive intelligence effort. Don't even think about it.

Assignment

1. What types of commercial photography appeal to you most?

2. Is there a niche within this type of commercial photography that you might exploit?

3. Assess the market for your preferred commercial photography specialty.

4. Conduct competitive analysis of those currently working in your preferred commercial photography specialty. What can you do that they cannot or do not? What can they do that you cannot?

8. Editorial Photography

Editorial photography documents the world in which we live and is used to illustrate written material in magazines, newspapers, websites, television, educational media, and other outlets. It is considered distinct from commercial photography which is used to sell products and services. Due to the association of editorial photography with journalism and photojournalism, there are often strict rules regarding the manipulation of photographs used for editorial purposes. There is also some relaxation of rules governing the use of a person's likeness compared to commercial photography. Examples of editorial photography include news photos, photo essays such as appeared in Life Magazine, photographs of insects in an insect guide, and photographs illustrating medical procedures in a nursing textbook.

Just as one might seek to establish a niche within commercial photography, one might also specialize in a certain area of editorial photography. For instance, one photographer might photograph extreme close-ups of insects (photomacrographs), while another might photograph birds, or even a certain species of bird. Another might specialize in the energy industry and only photograph alternative energy power plants such as wind farms. There are many specialists working in sports photography who may service a very narrow and distinct niche such as Formula 1 racing.

One thing to note is the low budget of many publications and other consumers of editorial imagery which might make it difficult to make a living as an editorial photographer, so doing your research on potential markets is essential. One might use the publication of images to build credibility for other photographic business pursuits. It is not uncommon for published nature photographers to offer photography workshops. A food photographer might get food photos published in order to increase his visibility to those seeking food photography for commercial uses. There is often some spillover between commercial and editorial photographers such that commercial photographers sometimes handle editorial assignments and editorial photographers sometimes shoot commercial assignments. Editorial photography, particularly news photography, is similar to wedding photography in that there is little room for error and usually no recourse for a reshoot if things don't go right, whereas commercial photographers usually have more control of the environment and have the ability to stage and execute a shot.

Consumers of Editorial Photography

Users of editorial photography include publishers of books, magazines, and websites; blogs, which often use stock imagery; news organizations, which are keen to purchase exclusive coverage of important events; non-government organizations (NGOs), which need photos that show the work they do and demonstrate their need for support; and any organization that needs to illustrate information that they are providing. Annual report photography is a special case that tends to bridge the gap between commercial and editorial photography. These photographs are editorial in the sense that they are used in articles that show the company's mission, yet they are commercial in the sense that they are used to sell investors on the future of the company. Composition, color, and textures often come together in a rich tapestry in an annual report.

Opportunity for Writers

If you are a writer then you should consider doing both writing and photography. Publishers often pay much better rates for a complete piece containing both the article and photographs for a magazine. A feature is a lead story in a magazine and these often pay the most. Books such as Writers Market and Photographers Market provide leads to magazines accepting proposals and the rates that they pay.

Finding Editorial Work

Where you look for assignments is dependent on the type of editorial photography you intend to pursue. You need a portfolio of work of the type you would like to shoot, and that should be your initial goal. Don't look for assignments of free work for building your portfolio. Instead, give yourself an assignment and a deadline. For instance, if you are planning to be a food photographer then you might give yourself an assignment to shoot a fruit dish today and have the image ready for publication tomorrow by noon. Do this type of assignment repeatedly until you have a great portfolio of impactful images. Increase the scope and complexity of the images as your skills improve, then add pressure by moving the deadlines tighter. Then you are ready to approach buyers. You can make this a doubly productive process by creating a portfolio along a theme in order to produce sufficient material for a book. Then publish the book through one of the print on demand publishers such as Blurb or Kindle Direct Publishing. Use the book as a presentation piece for potential clients. The fact that you did not use a traditional publisher is of less importance today as indie publishing becomes a means for writers to increase their share of the sales revenue from their books. Traditional publishers no longer control the distribution channel which was a major obstacle to self-publishing. Today you can distribute your works alongside those from traditional publishers on Amazon and let the market decide who has the superior product.

Many photographers promote their work via a specialty website dedicated to the niche they are trying to promote. For instance, a bird photographer might host a bird photography blog and write articles pertaining to areas of interest of bird photographers.

A food photographer might host a site dedicated to food photography or to images of food, i.e. show off the best of food photography. Some photographers create images for their portfolio and then register those images with a stock image vendor. This can provide a small income stream for niche images, but don't think of it as anything other than a small amount of supplemental income. More generic photo sharing sites such as Instagram work well for generating leads and contacts.

If you are planning to sell your work to news publications then you will need to contact the editors of those publications to introduce them to your work. It helps to have a strong portfolio of current work of the type they publish. Assignment work is make or break, if you don't produce great work on every assignment your assignments will dry up since the editors will stop giving them to you. Keep cultivating relationships with editors of publications having larger readership than you currently have. It's OK to start small, everyone has to start somewhere. But there is no need to get stuck in a rut with one publication.

A great way to make yourself known is to create your own assignment to cover something newsworthy to which no one else is paying attention, then put forth a great public relations effort to announce the finished work on social and traditional media. You want national media coverage if possible, although in some cases your project may have only regional interest. A project of national interest may be local to you, so don't discount things happening in your own locale.

Non-government Organizations (NGOs) often need coverage of their activities to help raise funds for their operations. If you plan to travel to an area where they perform their mission be sure to contact as many as you can and try to get assignments. You can often combine assignments on a single trip. As with much editorial work the pay may not be great but you gain an opportunity to produce images for your portfolio that you might otherwise not get. At the same time you may be able to produce stock images for an additional income stream, and perhaps one or more books. Although an NGO might have enough work to keep you busy for an entire trip, it's worth investigating multiple assignments among various organizations which have a presence in the area to which you will be traveling.

Independent publishing has gained credibility over the past few years and often provides a better income stream than going through a traditional publisher. Consider pre-selling your books using Kickstarter. A Kickstarter campaign allows you to have access to funds to help you achieve your goal, gives you the freedom to accomplish your objective without having to worry about having sufficient funds of your own to complete it, and provides a customer base for the sale of your book. It's really a winning formula for a project providing you can get the sufficient number of backers. A common strategy is to create a number of contribution categories. The lowest categories might get a signed copy of your book, with higher level contribution levels advancing toward larger rewards such as an invitation to an opening party for the gallery show for the book as well as a signed print or portfolio. For instance, you might have several contribution levels for a project that will result in a book and a portfolio. The book might sell for $35 in a soft cover edition, $50 in a hardcover, and a print might sell for $100 with a portfolio of 12 prints selling for $1000. You might offer a $10 level for which the contributor might receive a certificate of appreciation, $35 level for a signed soft cover copy and a certificate of appreciation, $50 level for a hardcover edition and a certificate of appreciation, $150 level for a signed hardcover edition, a print, and a certificate of appreciation, a $1000 level for a portfolio, signed hardcover edition, and their name featured at your opening. You could add another higher level to include the $1000 level plus dinner with you at a nice restaurant.

Assignment

1. What types of editorial photography might you pursue?

2. How would you market your editorial photography services?

3. Write a story and illustrate it with your images.

4. Create an editorial assignment with specific image objectives and a deadline. Shoot and edit your images. Complete the assignment before your deadline. (Hint: Make the deadline challenging.)

9. Portrait Photography

Everywhere you look you see portraits. Images of family members will be found on desks at work, photos of children in wallets, family portraits on walls, headshots of business people and actors in various publications and promotional material. Many, if not most, are produced by professionals. Phones and small digital cameras are commonly used to record family events but when people need a more formal photograph or one for an important purpose such as a job application they tend to prefer to use the services of a professional portrait photographer.

There are many potential market niches for portrait photographers and it is possible to be successful in most of them even in relatively small markets. We can divide the market into subject areas such as Animals, Children, Teens, High School Seniors, Family, Newborns, Large Groups, and Headshots. Each of these niche markets has unique characteristics in how the images are created as well as how one markets to the potential clientele. Although it is sometimes difficult to establish a presence in multiple commercial photography specialties such as fashion and food, it is not so hard to pursue multiple specialties within portraiture. Often a photographer will handle both business portraits and additional specialties such as Seniors and Family portraiture. For much portraiture the lighting equipment, cameras, backgrounds, and other necessities are the same, so there is relatively little additional overhead required.

Animal Portraits

People love their pets and will often include a pet in the family portrait. Some take it a step further and have portraits made of their pets. For instance, a horse might be a thoroughbred that won an award or race. A dog might be one that won best in show or is being placed for stud. It might be an elderly dog who has been a loyal family member for many years. In some cases the pet may be the only family the owner has. Animals who are performers require a headshot or action shot just like actors.

Animal portraiture can be a lucrative niche. Although the dog show circuit and similar large operations may be out of reach for most entrepreneurs, a steady clientele should be within reach through marketing to breed groups, local publications, bulletin boards, and veterinarian offices, as well as social media advertising that targets pet owners in your locale. Seasonal events like Pet Photos With Santa and specials like Mutt Mondays can be used for promotions.

A studio is not an absolute requirement for animal portraiture. Many animal portraits are made outdoors. They may be posed or they may be action shots. Natural light supplemented with flash or reflectors often produces the most pleasing portraits. An assistant who positions reflectors and moves lights for you will be a big help in getting your job done quickly and efficiently, hopefully before the subject becomes uncooperative or the customer becomes frustrated. Think in terms of sales opportunities. Ask questions about the animal and try to ascertain whether there are any special things the animal does that you might capture in order to get a great image and to boost sales.

Child Portraiture

At one time there were a large number of portrait studios specializing in children's portraiture or whose success was largely associated with children's portraiture. This appears to be a relic of the past as we have seen the demise of the Sears Portrait Studios and similar operations. The rise of digital photography and the overhead compared to sales potential might be to blame, so one must tread carefully in this specialty in order to be successful. Finding an exclusive and high margin niche would appear to be essential. A fashion photography session in which the child is treated like a super model might be a successful approach in some markets like a high end mall in a wealthy suburb. Location photography shooting the child's "lifestyle" might be another. Very formal portraiture reflective of portraiture of long ago might be another. Anything that is easily replicated by a mother and her Canon Rebel should be avoided.

Divide your child portrait market into three segments - Young, Teen, and Seniors. The young and very young children have a ready market for low priced portraits for grandparents and other relatives, however this implies low margins unless you own the means of production and can print your own packages. The teen market is hard to crack but could be approached with unique marketing ideas such as the model shoot and lifestyle approaches mentioned previously. The Senior market is competitive and to do well you really need to blow the competition out of the water with something the Seniors will want in order to impress their friends. For instance, work something out with a travel agent to put together a chaperoned cruise or trip to a vacation resort. The Seniors would be photographed in a range of attire from swimsuits to formal wear. Make arrangements with hair stylists, make up artists, and clothing vendors to supply goods and services. The students taking such a trip will usually be competitive with each other in terms of purchasing additional goods and services, so the vendors should do well and you should be able to make a substantial margin on each sale. Put together a package that includes airfare, hotel or ship cabin, meals and entertainment, makeup and hair styling sessions, gift certificates from local boutiques, and a couple of fun side trips at the destination, as well as a package of photographs. Sell the exclusivity and uniqueness of the resulting photos. For a chaperone, take an assistant and perhaps one of the more liberal parents. Ask the kids who they think would make a good chaperone, you wouldn't want anyone on the trip who is going to spoil the fun for everyone. Some people assume kids are always up to no good and this isn't the type of person conducive to a fun and successful trip. Some ground rules like no drugs and booze are given. You want the kids to look their best in the photos and the hung over look isn't appealing at all. Keep the kids busy so there is no time for undesired extracurricular activities. For example, have an early morning trip to a fun destination. Then include a fun brunch, shopping trip or other activity for midday while the light is harsh. Then give everyone a couple of hours to get ready for an afternoon/evening shoot followed by a dinner and party. The goal is for the kids to have fun and come back with some incredible images. The girls will immediately associate this type of trip with a Sports Illustrated swimsuit issue shoot and the boys will have fun with it as well.

Photographers who market to students need a representative at each school to create a buzz for the studio. A good way to select a rep is to have a contest with the winner being named the top model for that school. Pay your rep a small stipend each month as well as a small commission on each sale that she generates. A popular girl at the school is your best marketing tool. If you organize a trip let this rep be your assistant to keep the others organized. She will also be your eyes and ears in the group and help you head off any problems before they get out of hand.

Use a reward system to bring in additional business by giving customers print credit for each sale they generate. For instance, give a $50 gift certificate to your products for a $250 sale. Make it substantial and worthwhile to those who go to the effort or you will not see much in the way of sales from this approach.

Family Portraits

There is still a market for family portraits but true success in this area comes from the sale of large prints. Formal portraits that are well composed, with the family wearing nice clothing that is color coordinated works best for this type of photograph. A popular approach for photographers near the ocean is a photograph of the family in the sand dunes. Sure, it's trite and overdone but people like the images. If you are more inland then a nice meadow works well. Most municipalities have a suitable park for family portraits. Shoot early in the day if at all possible for best light and so that everyone is comfortable and not suffering from the heat of the day. Another popular location is a formal living room. Photographers who have a studio can pose the family against a hand painted formal backdrop.

An alternative approach for family portraiture is lifestyle photography. This is a good approach for active families, such as those who enjoy sailing on their boat. You would accompany them on the boat and photograph them sailing, then put the group together for a shot on the boat. This can lead to a sizable order including a large group portrait and a number of smaller images of each family member as part of the crew. Lifestyle portraits don't have to be limited to adventure or sporting activities. A farm family could just as well be photographed using a similar approach. Look at the lifestyles common to those in your market and try to see past the tired methods of the past and look to new and fresh approaches that will appeal to those in your market. Think in terms of exclusive, marketable niches.

When presenting images for sale, it helps if you can show the images in a large size, so a projector would be an asset. Some photographers have a large frame mounted on the wall in their sales office and project the image inside the frame in order to show how the photograph would look on the wall. If you make sales presentations to people in their homes a pico projector might prove useful. They are very portable yet project a nice bright image.

Newborn Portraits

There are a few photographers whose niche is photography of newborns. These may be taken at the hospital or in-home. In some instances you might contract with a hospital to provide services. There is a ready market for photographs. Providing a package that appeals to most customers, being able to deliver in a timely manner, and maintaining a high close rate for the number you shoot is essential. This can be a competitive market while being a challenging type of photography to do well.

Group Portraits

Another specialty within portraiture is the group portrait. The high end of this market is provision of very large and detailed photographs of a group of a large number of people. This is usually accomplished through the use of a large format camera (8x10 or larger) or by shooting multiple exposures and stitching them together, panorama style. This being so specialized it might be possible for you to collaborate with other photographers who handle event coverage but who do not have the equipment for the large groups. Needless to say you should only deal with photographers who have a very high respect for quality, anyone else may be too protective of his business to take advantage of your capability. Your market for large group portraits extends to family reunions, company functions, and large social events. Send a postcard to the HR departments of large companies in your area to let them know you are available to shoot such large groups. Research family reunions to find out who is planning a large one. If a large social event is being held that lends itself to a large group portrait then reach out to the organizers.

Headshots

Headshots are a specialty product that are needed by business people, models, and actors. A good headshot photographer can make a very good income doing only headshots. A good headshot photographer is one who can capture the essence of the subject while making subjects feel at ease in front of a camera. Being a good conversationalist who can think of relevant questions to ask really helps. When you engage your subject in conversation they tend to drop the facade they tend to adopt when getting prepared for the camera. Most headshots are done in a studio. Sometimes a headshot photographer will have a portable studio to handle an assignment to shoot a busy executive. Occasionally you might shoot a more environmental portrait, such as the executive sitting on the corner of her desk.

Niches in Portraiture

As we can see there are a number of specialties within the genre of portraiture, however we can further subdivide these and create specific niches. The way to do this is to take a specialty and ask what types of photography might be represented in that specialty, then subdivide those further. When you do this you might identify a niche that no one has really thought of as a photographic specialty, but which you can leverage for increased sales by becoming the "go to" person for that specialty. Then you can promote yourself as that expert. Small niches like this are of interest to reporters looking for human interest stories, so they can become a means of getting some free publicity. If you buy advertising from a newspaper or magazine then be sure to try to negotiate an article about you and your business as part of the deal.

Here are some examples. Within animal photography we might ask what types of animals, and immediately dogs come to mind. There are many classifications of dogs, such as show dogs, puppies, performers, and mutts. Thinking about this from a marketing perspective, perhaps we recognize that most dogs are mutts and mutts typically don't get the attention that purebred dogs get, therefore we come up with the idea of "Mutt Mugs", a business specializing in photographing mutts. This approach can be applied to developing any special niche. In the prior example of lifestyle photography we considered a farming family as a lifestyle subject. This would be a great niche in family oriented farming communities, for instance in Nebraska. In some areas you are more likely to find a cattle ranch than a farm, so again you have an excellent lifestyle niche. Since many farming communities are small you might have difficulty in maintaining an excellent income stream by limiting your services to that community. However, you could travel to a number of communities in your area. Advertise in the local newspaper when you are coming to town and try to pre-arrange bookings. Digital photography allows you to shoot, prepare a sales presentation with images from the shoot, and close the sale all within a few hours. You could post process images and place your orders for customer prints in your hotel room that evening. Take advantage of the technology that you have at your disposal. Within the specialty of headshots there are a number of niches one might pursue, for instance C-suite Executives. These are the CEOs and other chief officers who need strong images to go with annual reports and corporate information pages on websites. You need to be able to work quickly, capture great images, and have flawless execution. You need a personality that is not intimidated by executives. A great sense of humor will help you a long way in this regard.

Assignment

1. What types of portraiture would you do and why?

2. How would you market your portrait photography services?

3. Create a portrait of a subject of the type you would like to photograph professionally. Try to think outside the box and be very creative. How might you improve your results?

10. Event Photography

Many photographers make a good living shooting events. This type of photography usually refers to photographing events such as family reunions and weddings which provide an often rare opportunity for family members to get together. Consequently, they provide a means for photographers to provide photographs of family members together on these rare occasions. This is an incredible sales opportunity for photographers who photograph events with sales in mind. For instance, if a relative comes a long distance to attend the event it is unlikely photographs of family members with that relative may be made again anytime soon. Therefore, one would want to be sure to get plenty of images of that person with other family members in various combinations.

Online sites now make it easy for your customers to order photos from you. Providing an online catalog of images and order form makes it easy for customers to order images after they return home. This has an added benefit of removing the responsibility for order management from the client. If you incur no extra expense by doing so, then by all means leave the order pages up indefinitely since people tend to procrastinate about ordering photos. People have various priorities, some might want to order right away while others may not get around to it for months. By removing the management responsibilities from your client you have an opportunity to create an income stream from the event lasting months or even years. Some photographers make sales at the event, printing and delivering the orders that day. Even if you take that route you can increase your sales by also providing an online catalog.

Events offer no room for error. You must have reliable equipment and multiple backups of equipment and supplies. If you can take a failure in stride and move to your substitute equipment then you should be able to maintain a productive workflow and complete the assignment successfully. Essential equipment should have at least two backups. Look at every piece of equipment you use down to the batteries and cables and verify that you can handle failures effectively. Have things stored and labeled in an orderly manner so that the replacement is easy to find and there is no doubt that you have the correct replacement. Think through emergency procedures so that you don't lose an important shot when a failure occurs. For instance, you might switch to a higher ISO and shoot natural light while your assistant retrieves the backup flash unit if your primary flash dies. Use a checklist to verify that you have every piece of equipment you need before you leave for the event and that every piece of equipment has been properly tested. In the film days we would verify not only that the shutter speed was set to properly sync with the flash, but that the curtain travel was correct and the entire curtain was out of the way when the flash fired. This was a critical check because there was no instant feedback like we have today. Consider your situation and determine whether you are exposed to any risks that would be difficult to detect during a shoot. For instance, a smudge on a lens could be disastrous, yet difficult to detect while shooting.

You must maintain control of every event that you shoot. Your contract should prohibit others from shooting your setups. This is a distraction to everyone involved and will ruin your images. Ask anyone with a camera to refrain from shooting until you are completely through your setups. That includes people with cell phones who are often the worst offenders. If possible ask everyone who is not going to be in the photographs to leave the area temporarily. You can call attention to those ruining your images if you do so in a humorous manner and it might motivate someone in the group to tell the offender to put the camera away. For instance, "Oh no, that's no good. We have some people looking at the camera and some looking at Aunt Martha over there. I know she's better looking than me, maybe we should stand her right here."

Family Reunions

There are various types of family reunions, ranging from small family gatherings with three or four generations to very large events attended by everyone with a common surname. The latter might have hundreds of people attending.

As an event increases in size the logistics of photographing and sales become more complicated. For very large events you might need multiple photographers as well as a process in place for taking orders and keeping track of who you photograph. You can keep a slate with you to record names and other info which you can shoot before and/or after each setup. Add other identifying information as needed. A portable payment collection device such as an iPhone with a credit card scanner may allow you to collect payments as you shoot. An assistant can help with the payment logistics while letting you focus on shooting.

Another approach that would eliminate the need to keep track of which images are associated with specific orders would be to issue a unique identifier such as a receipt number and let the customer order anything on the online catalog. Each receipt would represent a credit for the amount of the purchase. If the customer didn't like how her image turned out she could order an alternate. The benefit of this approach is that you can generate cash flow on the front end of the project.

Make sure you hand out cards and other information on ordering. If there is a website for the event then ask the person in charge to add your contact info and the order info to the website. This is also a good opportunity to use social media to establish and maintain relationships with the attendees in order to facilitate sales. If most of the attendees live in your market locale then you have a tremendous marketing opportunity at your disposal.

Weddings

When most people think of event photography they think of weddings. Oddly, it seems that most beginning photographers do wedding photography as their first photographic business venture. This often results in disaster since the inexperienced have no concept of the finer points of wedding photography and they are usually one mistake away from ruining the entire wedding. The bride is often lucky to get some poorly exposed snapshots. There are three important aspects to successful wedding photography. First is the technical and creative capabilities of the photographer. Next is the ability of the photographer to control the event and work with people. Third is business and marketing acumen. You must master all three to be successful in this field. There are classes on these aspects, but many of the business and marketing classes are big on hype and small on substance, often promising riches to the photographer simply by raising his prices. General marketing and business training may be a better investment, so do your research first before spending a lot of money on a wedding marketing course. Talk to others who have taken the course and ask them if the investment was worth it and whether they implemented any of the advice given. If they are enthusiastic in their recommendation then it might be a worthwhile course. In terms of the technical and creative side, find someone whose work you like a lot for your instructor. It's difficult to adapt a particular style to a different visual approach. An instructor may be well regarded but if you don't like the type of imagery he or she produces then it may be a waste of your time and money.

Just as in any other event photography you should photograph with sales in mind. Use every photographic opportunity to produce an additional image the client will want. Although your customer may have contracted for an album and a couple of enlargements, there is a huge sales opportunity for additional prints to the bride and groom, family members, friends, etc. Think outside the shot list.

There are often several vendors involved in a wedding. Providing them copies of photos of their work featured at the event helps you build rapport with these vendors and is a great way to generate additional sales via word of mouth. Customers take advice from vendors who they trust.

Niches in Events

Always be on the lookout for a special niche you can exploit in the event field. Given the competition you face in most types of event photography, anything you can do to differentiate yourself from the crowd has potential benefit. For instance, if you photograph large family reunions you might consider adding a large format camera, panoramic camera, or Gigapan style camera to your arsenal. This would permit you to produce very detailed images of people in a large group photo, thereby facilitating sales of larger images of these groups. This is an important selling point when booking a large reunion. Examples showing the output from different types of cameras would drive the point home. You don't have to tell the customer that your competitor uses an inferior technology, you just have to demonstrate that what you use is better. Simply owning the equipment does not instantly grant you the expertise to deliver a quality product. You must practice with it until you have mastered the techniques required of the technology you intend to employ. This includes mastering the techniques of post-processing. If you use multiple images to create panoramic group portraits you may need to blend images to remove movement or other defects.

People love the unusual and unique. Give them something to brag about to their friends. Black and white film photography makes an interesting niche because the photographs have a special appeal and the negatives and silver prints have an incredibly long life, making this an excellent choice for shooting family reunion and similar events where the images may become family heirlooms.

The stronger your niche the fewer clients you have in a given market, generally speaking. However, customers in search of specialists within a niche category will be more likely to seek you out, so making sure you are easy to find is essential. This means at least minimal participation in social networks and maintaining your website. A site that looks like it hasn't been touched in 10 years is a bit of a turn off for some. Consider expanding your market in order to gain a major foothold on the niche you pursue. Become the "go to" person regionally or even nationwide.

Practice makes perfect. Look for opportunities to practice your niche in challenging situations. Then, publish the results in media that will garner attention from your target market.

Conclusion

Event photography can be lucrative and large companies have been built servicing this segment of the photographic market. It's not for everyone. You must like dealing with people and have a take charge attitude. You also need to be detail oriented, be able to think on your feet, and the capability to be flexible when things don't go as planned.

Assignment

1. Does event photography appeal to you? If so, what type of events would you like to photograph professionally?

2. Create a plan to begin photographing events. What would be a good type of event to start with?

3. How would you market your event photography services?

11. Your Business Plan

Many people start a business without any consideration of their customer acquisition strategy, billing rates for their services, funding of capital expenditures, or even how they will make payroll during their startup phase. They may fail to develop a plan to pursue their intended market, resulting in a lack of direction. As a result they tend to seek any assignment that they can find, undercharging for their work, buying equipment they don't need, spending money on advertising that doesn't work, spending even more money on website SEO and other gimmicks, and finally giving up. A business plan is simply an organized way of looking at the many factors that affect your business and preparing to run your business in a way that takes those into account. You probably don't need a full-fledged business plan unless you are submitting a loan application to the SBA or similar organization, but it's a good idea to formulate at least a basic plan. You need to understand the market you intend to pursue, capitalize your business so that it can stay afloat while you create a stream of new customers, create a legal entity that best supports your business and financial goals, and establish targets and metrics for measuring your success. I like to compare creation of a business with building a house. You can build a house without a set of plans, however you are more likely to wind up with a shack than a house. Look around you and you will see that the most successful businesses are those that dominate a particular niche. This doesn't occur by chasing every idea that comes along.

Part Time vs. Full Time

In many cases a business is being started with extremely limited funds due to the lack of capital and the inability or unwillingness to borrow money. Sometimes the business owner doesn't see the business as creating sufficient income to be a full time commitment. For whatever reasons, it is often necessary to create the business as a part time enterprise. Be careful with your assumptions since it is easily possible to wind up with full time commitments in your part-time pursuit. Don't underestimate the time requirements for the various aspects of running your business. There is also a tendency to settle for less in terms of your creative fee when you are shooting part time. Don't do it. If you are feeling charitable then why bother with the business at all? Just provide your services for free. There should be plenty of willing takers. If on the other hand you do intend to make a business of it then charge your clients a fee that makes it worth your time and effort to do a great job. Quoting the client a cheap price is a disservice to the client because it increases the tendency for you to take shortcuts and compromise quality since the client "is only paying $xxx." When you charge what the product and service is really worth you will be more inclined to put forth the extra effort required to do a great job for your client.

Your Cost of Doing Business

There are a number of important calculations you need to make as part of your business plan. One of these is your cost of doing business (CODB). However, contingent on this calculation is another calculation, your cost of living. Unless you have another income stream on which you can reliably depend, part of your CODB is the salary you need in order to cover your living expenses. This is no time to cheat and underestimate this cost; if you have an expense that is not taken into account you are going to have to come up with the shortage at some point. Everything needs to go into the CODB calculation including equipment, supplies, rent and utilities, advertising, telephone, internet, web site design and hosting, software, travel, meals, etc. I often see people asking questions on internet forums regarding deducting equipment expenses. This is the type of question best asked of an accountant, which we will discuss later on in this chapter, however the short answer is that you will account for and deduct every single expense to which you are entitled, not just equipment purchases. Some expenses occur infrequently, such as a camera purchase, while other may occur very regularly such as salary and travel. Estimate these as best you can. Again, don't cheat and underestimate the numbers as this will come back and bite you later.

Risk Analysis and Mitigation

Risk analysis is a highly useful tool for making business decisions. I've found that a simple procedure called Qualitative Risk Analysis does more to assist decision making than any other business process. It consists of three basic steps:

1. Create a list of risk factors and assign each a probability of occurrence of 1, 2, or 3 which will correlate to low, medium, or high probability.

2. For each risk factor assign each an impact value of 1, 2, or 3 which will correlate to low, medium, or high impact.

3. For each risk factor multiply the probability by the impact. If the product is 4 or more then you should consider steps to mitigate the risk.

Let's do one as an example. One risk for a wedding photographer is that he will accidentally erase all the pictures of the wedding or some other disaster will occur which results in all of the pictures being destroyed, resulting in the bride and groom suing for damages. Things like this happen often enough, particularly with new photographers, so I'd score this a 2 for medium risk of occurrence. The impact of a lawsuit is potentially very high, so I'd score the impact as a 3. The product of 2x3 is 6, which is greater than the level at which we require mitigation. There-fore, we would take steps to mitigate the risk. There are a number of ways we might mitigate, or handle, the risk. First, we might purchase liability insurance to protect us against a lawsuit. Second, we might establish a business process for handling recording media to reduce the risk of data destruction, since we would rather not get to the point of needing to use that insurance. For instance, we might require that media be backed up as soon as possible after it is removed from the camera and that it be kept segregated pending backup. We might require that a full checksum be made on both the storage media and on the backup media before erasing a data card. We might make data cards part of the project esti-mate and never erase them, instead using the data card for one of the backups. The business processes we implement to reduce risk should be documented and made company policy. In some instances this business process might be used to reduce the rate paid for errors and omissions (E&O) insurance. The implementation of a company policy involves training employees with respect to that policy. Always verify that employees have been trained by testing their knowledge of your policies and perform spot checks on occasion to confirm compliance. Some employees mean well but never learn to adhere to policies. They should be reassigned to less risky positions in the company or else terminated.

Whenever you make a business decision ask yourself first which risk factors are involved. Often you can avoid much analysis and decision making by realizing a risk factor exists that makes the decision easy. If you perform a serious risk analysis of everything you do in your business you may find that many of your business processes will pretty much write themselves as risk mitigation strategies.

Market Research

An investor once listened to a passionate group of entrepreneurs describe the product they were developing. His response was interesting. "It's easy for some people to sit in a room and convince themselves they have a great idea." It was sort of a polite way of saying "This pig won't fly." This is true of many photography entrepreneurs who think they will have the world by the tail and will make a killing as a highly paid photographer. The reality is often far from it. In order to avoid a business failure you should research the market for your products and services. It may be that there is simply not enough business in the market you have defined that is sufficient to support you. This could arise from a number of conditions ranging from the amount of competition to the level of interest in the products and services that you sell. Often a niche must be developed, but the requirement for a market still exists. There are various types of market research that you can employ. Some measures are statistical in nature, such as the number of wedding licenses issued per year. Some might require surveying a sample of potential customers. In some cases you can look at successful ventures in similar markets. Customize your market research for your genre. If you are a commercial photographer specializing in food then look at the number of restaurants and other potential customers. Examine their current use of photography. Can it be better? Is it nonexistent, and if so, why? Use as many sources of information as you can find. Your library might have past years of the local newspaper that you can analyze for seasonal photographic usage. Government agencies might have statistical information of interest. Get out in the field and talk to potential clients. Ask restaurant owners why they don't use photos, or if they do use photos ask them what impact they have had on sales.

Use realistic assumptions in your assessments of the data that you examine. Not every wedding will have a wedding photographer. Many restaurants are barely surviving and can little afford photography services. When you interview potential clients, pose realistic questions and use qualifiers. Why haven't you used photography in your advertising? What would a good photograph be worth to you? Do you have plans to increase your advertising budget? Wedding photographers might ask similarly qualified questions. Did you hire a professional photographer for your wedding? What is a fair price for a photographer? What should you get for that amount? What didn't you like about your wedding photographer? Use the opportunity to not only test your market hypothesis, but to find additional information that you might use in your advertising to increase your sales.

In some locales seasonality is an important criteria. For instances, if 80 percent of the weddings occur in May and June then you may need a very high creative fee to make your business carry you through the year or else you may need other types of income during the slow months.

Startup Expenses

The old adage "It takes money to make money" is true. However, another adage that is just as important does not get repeated as frequently, "Preservation of capital is key." One of the biggest mistakes new entrepreneurs make is failure to control their expenses, often spending wildly on equipment and other items that they think they will need. Preservation of capital is the single most important factor in staying in business. Always maintain cash reserves. Only buy what you need. If you think that you might need something on an ongoing basis but you aren't sure, see if you can rent it. Don't squander your capital. Also, be careful that you don't underestimate the amount of money you'll need to stay in business. For instance, if you are a wedding photographer who is busy during the wedding season in March through September, but then the business drops off precipitously during the late Fall and Winter, you will need funds to support you during that slow time. Some photographers have a second location where others migrate during the slow season, for instance shooting weddings in New Jersey in the warm months and shooting portraits in Palm Beach during the Winter.

Most photographers who are starting a business already own some equipment, however some types of photography require backup equipment to assure the photographer's ability to successfully complete a job in the case a piece of equipment breaks down. Often the backup equipment is sufficient to serve in an emergency even if it isn't what you would normally use for a job. When you perform your risk analysis take into account the risk of different types of equipment breakdown and develop a mitigation strategy that permits you to carry on despite adversity.

The amount of money you need to start and stay in business varies according to too many factors to consider here. If after adding everything up you don't see any way to obtain the amount of funds you will need, think seriously about changing your startup strategy. Don't just plow ahead in hope that things will work out in your favor, since extra expenses and timing issues always crop up and tend to negatively impact even the best laid plans. Ideally, if you intend to immediately go full time, you should plan on having from 6 months to a year's worth of savings that you can rely on while building the business. If you are starting part-time then this isn't as much of an issue since you have your regular income to rely upon. One thing to keep in mind with respect to part time work, you need to make sure you can schedule things so as not to conflict with your regular job, whether taking vacation time or working on your time off.

Advertising

Advertising and marketing your business is critical if you are to be successful in your business. There are a number of methods available to you ranging from simple word of mouth, the Internet via social media and websites, as well as guerilla approaches that expose your business to potential customers in unique and effective ways. The traditional approach to advertising was an advertising campaign that might be executed in local print media as well as radio and television. This is still possible, however in many instances print media has lost readership, radio has become a wasteland populated with extremists, and television channels suffer from so much competition there are few places it might be considered worthwhile. Targeted social media campaigns can be more effective for some types of photography. Membership and sponsorship of organizations to which your potential customers belong can be an effective marketing opportunity.

Word of mouth advertising is how the majority of sales are made in many areas. If people are happy with the products and service they received then they tend to brag to their friends about it. The people who hear about it often repeat the information to their friends if they hear of someone with a need for a similar product or service. Therefore, it pays to implement strategies that increase word of mouth advertising for your business. Note that price information is also passed along, which tends to limit your ability to raise your prices. It's nearly always a better practice to offer something extra in your bid than to cave in on pricing and give discounts. One reason that it is a particularly bad idea to give discounts is that it immediately provides the impression that your prices must have been too high to start with. Additionally, customers will forever after expect the same discount on future orders.

Print Advertising

Print advertising is usually done in local newspapers and magazines. Repetition is important. A single ad may get a few responses, but a regularly appearing ad is much more effective as your name comes to mind when the need for your services is realized. Most newspapers will work with you to come up with a discounted insertion period for testing your ad. For instance in a daily paper you might run an ad on Wednesday and Sunday for eight weeks. An offer specific to that ad can be used to indicate the effectiveness of that particular ad, particularly when you are running multiple ads in various publications. It's important to know which ads are effective and which are not so that you know which ones to continue running after the trial period.

Web Advertising

There are several Web advertising strategies you might employ. Some are free and others can be very expensive. The question to keep in mind is, how many people in my market are going to see my ad? This can be as simple as putting the city in the title field of pages in your website, like "Joe Barton - San Jose, CA Commercial Photographer". This simple change can result in a huge increase in search engine ranking. Local news sources sell advertising on their websites that may or may not be effective. Google AdWords can be effective but you need to carefully construct the search filters used so as to limit the amount of money spent on showing ads to people not in your market.

Guerilla Marketing

Guerilla marketing is a name given to unusual advertising approaches. These non-traditional techniques might include things like using QR codes to lead people your website, flyers in coffee shops, late night cable TV advertising, creating memes by using actors to talk about your products in a public context, using puzzles in classified ads to stir interest, and other techniques. Try to come up with methods of making contact with your target market by any means possible.

Social Media

Social media allows you to employ the public in driving your message. If you can create a message that is spread among members of networks you can reach a large number of people with little overhead. For instance, if you have a giveaway that requires participants to "like" you on Facebook, then those who see that like status might become interested and take a look at what you have to offer, thus creating contact that you might otherwise not have. Those interested in what you have to offer might follow you on Twitter if you regularly publish something of interest related to your products and services. It is easy to make a nuisance of yourself on social media. Most folks don't use it to see ads. They tend to tolerate ads, but when the commercial communications become overbearing they tend to change their usage patterns or make other modifications to filter your message. That might mean that they stop following you or similar measures. Therefore, make your participation in social media and engagement of others something enjoyable and rewarding from their perspective. One approach is to provide useful information, for instance a guide to working with your wedding photographer.

Networking and Shoe Leather Marketing

Sometimes you are better off getting out and meeting those who may be in need of your services or who can provide leads to those who do. For instance, wedding photographers need to get out and meet other wedding services vendors who can be a great source of leads. Networking events can introduce you to those needing photographic services. If you are trying to get started in fashion photography then you might find it useful to attend events targeting make up artists, fashion designers, and similar interests. Think about your buyer and her interests. Where will she go to interact with others in her field socially?

Specialized Marketing Sites

In certain photography genres like advertising photography there are portfolio oriented sites such as Workbook[1] that permit you to post work that might garner the attention of those looking for the type of work you do. The jury is out on whether these are still effective. In years past there were large black books containing the work on photographers and other creatives that were sent to ad agencies which provided an easy means of getting work in front of a lot of potential clients. Today, aside from reputation, a web search might turn up information on your photography with less effort than a search on one of these sites. For example, if you specialized in shots

---

1 http://www.workbook.com

of beverages being poured you would probably find it worth the effort to create an exception website of such images and then work on getting your site to come up in the top of search ranking for a reasonably representative search phrase. When you target a specific niche it is much easier to gain that ranking than if you are a generalist in a sea of SEO optimized mediocrity.

Advertising Summary

In terms of your business plan you should arrive at a budget estimate of the first year advertising expenditures. Analyze the different approaches available to you and develop a plan that incorporates those that you think will most likely result in sales. Then determine the budget required to implement those strategies.

Production Expenses

There are a number of costs associated with running a business. Some are one time or rarely occurring expenses such a equipment purchases, some are regularly occurring expenses like rent and utilities, and some are directly related to the products and services that you sell, such as the cost to produce a print. When you examine the products that you intend to sell, take into careful consideration the production costs of these goods. Include the ancillary costs in this estimate. If you shoot 100 jobs over the lifetime of your camera, and that camera cost $3000, then you have in effect a $30 expense per job just for the camera. You should include other expenses as well, such as the insurance you buy to protect your business against loss. It's OK to calculate a rough estimate since you never know what the true lifetime of equipment is going to be or what your insurance rates might be in the future. Estimate a little on the high side and you should be covered.

Whenever you produce something to be sold like a print, there is always a risk of loss or damage, or a mistake might be made by you or someone on your staff. Take the probability of this occurring in your pricing strategy. This is simply another of your risk calculations. Assume that every so often, something will happen that will result in you having to pay for a new print or other product that you sell. Build that cost into your pricing model.

Legal and Financial Advice

There are two professionals you need to make a permanent part of your business team, a certified public accountant (CPA) and an attorney. There is often a lot of fear that new business owners seem to have of these professionals. However, they will make your business more money over time than if you don't have them on your team.

Your Financial Team

A CPA has passed a very rigorous examination in order to become licensed and should be an expert on the financial aspects of your business pertaining to business entity formation and taxation. Your CPA will advise you on these matters and make sure you do all of the tax reporting that you are required to do for your business. A common question people have is whether they should form a corporation, sole proprietorship, or LLC, and they usually cast this in terms of risk from a lawsuit. There is a common perception that a business entity will magically shield one from a lawsuit. This is really the wrong question. Risk mitigation is only one of the reasons for deciding on a business entity type. There are others, such as tax reporting requirements, tax treatment of income, retirement account strategies, handling of medical expenses and insurance, and many others. Your CPA should help you perform a thorough analysis of all factors leading to the right decision for your circumstances.

Your Legal Team

Photographers need two attorneys, an IP attorney who can help assure that they protect their intellectual capital, the images they produce. The other is a business attorney who can provide input on the legal risk aspects of business entity choice and will help in the creation of contracts, negotiating contracts such as leases, etc. Attorneys typically work on a per project basis. When you need help with something you contact them with your specific requirements. Consider for example a situation in which you have created images for your stock library and you would like to license them. You need a license that protects your intellectual property. Your contract might state that your images are to be used for some specific purpose, in a particular market, and for a period of time and that you are receive some amount of compensation for this license. The best leverage you have is your copyright, and you can make the licensing contingent on payment. You will want to make sure that you register your copyrights in order to be able to file a lawsuit in the event your image is stolen. Your attorneys are your team in creating the contracts and copyright strategy to protect your interests. Can you do this without an attorney? Maybe, but you risk making an error that results in you losing a lawsuit, and you will need the IP attorney in the event you need to file a lawsuit. Consider another fairly common scenario in which another photographer steals your images and uses them to promote his business. Let's say you watermark your images. If you had registered your copyright it is very likely you could recover significant damages from the offending photographer. Likewise if your image had been stolen and used in an ad campaign by a corporation. Removal of watermarks opens the door for additional damages through the Digital Millennium Copyright Act (DMCA).

On any day nearly any Internet photography interest group will contain an article from someone complaining about the theft of images. The common thread on most of these is the failure of the photographer to register his copyright and as a result dilute not only his compensation, but also his ability to retain legal counsel to pursue damages. Don't let this be you.

Formal Business Plan

In many cases such as when applying for a business loan one needs to formulate a formal business plan. The Small Business Administration facilitates many business loans and the business plan structure that follows their guidelines is recommended for such cases. The SBA publishes an online guide[2] to writing your business plan which contains recommendations for the structure of the plan whether you have an existing business or a startup.

Execute the Plan

Think of your business plan as your road map for your business. Read it occasionally to remind yourself of your objectives. Are you still on the path or did you take a detour? If you allow yourself to be sidetracked then regroup, reassess, and reformulate your plan if necessary.

2 https://www.sba.gov/writing-business-plan

Assignment

1. Create your business plan.

2. Ask the business people you know if there is a CPA they do business with who they can recommend. Set up a lunch meeting and discuss your business plan.

3. Perform a Web search for an attorney you might use to pursue a copyright infringement case. Read the material on the attorney's website. Are you taking the steps you need to in order to pursue litigation?

12. Equip Yourself

It is a common scenario for photographers who decide to go into business to start buying all sorts of expensive equipment without giving careful thought to what they really need to be successful with the type of work that is going to produce income. Equipment is expensive. Often you need to do a lot of work to pay for a single lens or other item and some items may be used so infrequently that there is little likelihood you will ever cover the cost. Buy only what you need to accomplish a task and only when renting is not an option. When you purchase equipment, buy the best quality that you can afford. Make sure that you have backups of all essential equipment and supplies, and make sure you test your equipment before taking it into the field on an assignment.

Buy Only What You Need

Who doesn't want to try new lenses and other equipment? It's human nature to do so. Often there is a buzz in the photographic community over some new technology or piece of gear. This is a meme talking. You can choose not to listen! Take a critical look at how that equipment purchase might really help your business. Will it be used once per year or would it get regular use? Will it save you time? Does it enable you to do something that your competitors can't do and which will cause your customers to hire you? Neat and cool don't pay the bills. Be careful not to overestimate the contribution that the purchase might make toward your bottom line. Be realistic in your assessment. An incorrect assessment can easily result in you spending money that would be better spent on other things that you really need and might contribute to a loss for your business.

Buy Quality

 The phrase "buy once, cry once" is apropos in equipment purchases. Equipment is expensive. You often have a choice of brands or quality within a brand. For example there are professional and amateur versions of cameras and lenses. More goes into the distinction than a label and some performance numbers. Often there will be differences in moisture resistance, reliability, and build quality. Equipment that fails on a job is bad for your success and damages your credibility if it prevents you from completing an assignment. Top quality equipment retains its resale value better than lower quality equipment. Consider buying gently used top quality equipment which often has the best resale value. A high quality used lens will probably bring you nearly the same amount that you paid for it, years after you bought it.

 You rarely need the very latest versions of cameras and other equipment. When you start to feel like you are missing out on something by not having the newest toy on the block remember that you are probably infected with a meme. A meme is similar to a virus but it's an idea that takes hold and spreads through a population. Marketers are very effective in creating memes that make you want the thing that they are selling. It may be started by someone posting about the product on a popular blog, then gets picked up by "thought leaders" on forums, and then spreads to the followers of these thought leaders. You never know which blog and forum thought leaders are paid by a manufacturer to generate interest in products.

Don't be persuaded by those who dismiss your photography because you don't shoot with the latest gear. Ask yourself who is doing the talking and do their images reflect an opinion worth consideration?

Have Backups

Mission critical equipment should have one or more backups when you are on assignment. Backups do not have to replicate the equipment they are backing up 100%. For instance, a lower version body or a zoom that covers the range of two primes can take over in an emergency. If the job absolutely requires some capability, make sure that capability is backed up. In some cases you might carry two backups, such as two spare flash units if you are photographing weddings. It is possible for a backup unit to fail. Be sure to also keep plenty of other spares on hand such as batteries, data cards, and other expend-ables. Running out of data space in the middle of an assignment can really ruin your day.

Test Everything

It's astounding how many people will show up at an assignment with new gear they haven't bothered testing. Their customers watch while they fumble with the gear trying to figure things out and rapidly lose confidence in the photographer's ability to do his job. There are two reasons to test your equipment. First, you need to understand how it will operate in the context in which you will deploy it. Secondly, testing lets you to discover issues that you can cor-rect before going on assignment. Use of most equip-ment implies a workflow. The more you practice with the equipment the clearer that workflow becomes. Ultimately, the operation of that equipment should become fairly effortless as you intuitively implement the associated workflow. Failure to practice means that you have to develop the workflow in the midst of an assignment. If this occurs in a high stress situ-ation you are much more likely to overlook an impor-tant component of the workflow, resulting in a mis-take and potentially blowing the assignment.

Do your testing well in advance of the shoot, not just before you are scheduled to leave since you will need time to resolve any issues that you find. You want ease and peace of mind when you head out on a shoot. If you are flustered and frustrated from trying to fix an issue then that may have a negative impact on your work. Make sure that you check screws and fittings on tripods and other equipment regularly. You don't want your expensive gear falling off a tripod because of a loose screw.

Use Checklists

Always use a checklist. There are two types of checklists that you should be using. The first is a list of equipment and other assets you take on your assignment. This checklist is used to verify that you have everything that you need and is also used when you pack up at the end of the shoot to verify that you have brought everything back. This checklist might also reference a procedure that must be followed, which brings us to the procedural checklist.

The second type of checklist is the procedural checklist that is used to perform operations such as setting a camera up for a particular type of shoot, configure a strobe, or similar multi-step operation. For instance, there might be a white balance check on the camera setup checklist which itself may have it's own procedure to follow. Keep your checklists in a small notebook so that they are easily referenced. Find a notebook to which you can easily add new pages as you develop new checklists.

Pilots use checklists for all operations associated with their aircraft. Many of these checklists are remembered using mnemonic devices such as a word where each letter represents a checklist item. Although this works, having the hard copy is essential for when one can't recall which operation is represented by a letter.

Assignment

1. Make a list of all equipment you own which cost over $100.

2. Which items on the list you created do you rarely or never use? Which ones have you never used?

3. Add up the approximate cost of the items you bought but rarely or never use.

4. Calculate the total expenditure on all of your equipment.

5. Divide the total in 3 by the total in 4 and multiply the result by 100. This is the percentage spent on equipment which you do not use.

6. Find a website where you can rent photographic equipment. Look up the items that you bought that you rarely or never used. How much would you have saved by renting each item for a week compared to purchasing it?

14. Show Your Work

It matters not which genre you choose nor which niche you intend to dominate, you need to make your work available to those to whom you intend to market your photography. Today there are numerous opportunities to show your work and you should leverage as many of these opportunities available to you in order to gain exposure to those who might become customers. There are both physical and online means of showing your work. Although "online" implies worldwide visibility, you can target your online presence in a way that makes sense for marketing to your locale. For instance, including locale information in your online presence increases the probability of your content being seen by those searching for local photographers in that medium, whether it be your own website, Flickr, Twitter, Tumblr, Instagram, or other outlet. Some local outlets to consider are galleries, coffee shops and restaurants, contests, pop-up shows, libraries, and other venues where images are commonly displayed. You might convince the owners of a venue that doesn't commonly display images to consider doing so to increase traffic or garner attention, particularly when your work is illustrative of or is in line with their objectives. If you are an art photographer or pursuing national or international presence then the larger contests and art shows might be on your list of contacts as well as magazines.

Flickr

Flickr is a good outlet for finding exposure to buyers of photographic images such as magazines and stock image agencies. Flickr is huge and features the work of many excellent photographers. As you add images to your Flickr portfolio you might think of groupings or categorizations that lends themselves to social media spin. Create a stir in your social media circles by posting a link to your new work.

Instagram

Instagram has become an excellent outlet for sharing your photography and gaining access to buyers. It may be surpassing Flickr in popularity, particularly among buyers of photography. Many new art photographers are getting their start through their activity on this social media platform. This is an interesting phenomenon considering its past association with the over-manipulation of images. Posting to Instagram should be regular and consistent. Don't surprise followers with work that doesn't support the theme or genre you are presenting.

Twitter

Twitter is great for keeping abreast of current events and for making announcements to drive traffic to your new work. Twitter has added photo sharing to the Twitter feed as well as video, so a representative image might be displayed with a link to additional work. Use hashtags to help your work be found by those who are not following your Twitter account. Reply to and retweet messages from high traffic sites to draw attention to your feed. Breaking news images are commonly posted to Twitter. In order to maintain full control of your rights, be sure to register your copyrights.

Facebook

Facebook provides many methods of getting in front of potential customers, from targeted advertising to special interest groups. It is a popular social media platform so should be part of most marketing strategies. Facebook allows you to send targeted advertising to specific demographics in your target market. An understanding of all the features of this platform is well beyond the reach of this book and finding an expert on the medium would be money well spent.

Coffee Shops

With the popularity of specialty coffee drinks there has been a great increase in the number of small coffee shops. Many of the shops feature the work of local artists on a rotating basis. Art photographers can often hang a show and sell work in such a venue. It is a step below a gallery show but a good way to get your work seen locally. In some cases you cannot gain exposure in publications without having shown your work, and starting with a small local show such as this might help you get a start.

Libraries

Libraries often have galleries and will host a show. The "gallery" might amount to a short stretch of wall. If the library is not conducive to a one-person show perhaps you could generate interest in a group show with other local artists. That show might have a theme based on something of local interest or an important anniversary.

Galleries

Most art photographers dream of getting gallery representation. Art galleries that feature photographic exhibits typically have interest in specific types of work. Do your research. On most gallery websites you should find a description of the type of work they look for as well as instructions for submitting a proposal. Make sure that your work falls within their guidelines and that you follow the instructions for submitting work. If you fail to do either of these you may assume that your submittal will be rejected.

A gallery might ask for exclusive representation and a high percentage of your sales. Ask what you are actually getting for that level of commitment. Will the gallery be aggressive in marketing your work?

How much of your time will be required to assist in these efforts? Who pays for framing or other presentation requirements? A great gallery will cultivate its artists and carefully increase the visibility and value of their work.

There are some galleries that let you rent space for your work. This can be useful if you want to hold a short show in an area with high traffic. For instance, some areas have a lot of nighttime activity on the weekend and will occasionally have an "art crawl" to generate more business for the local shops, restaurants, and bars. This is a good opportunity to get your work seen and also to make a few sales.

Corporate Offices

Corporations buy art to display in their lobbies, hallways, meeting rooms, and offices. Some corporations may regularly change the art, particularly in areas with a lot of public access such as large lobbies. Do your research. You may have to place a few phone calls to determine who handles procurement of the art being displayed. It may be handled in-house or contracted to an external interior design firm.

Universities

If your work might be of interest to those in a specific educational field of study, then consider showing the work to the appropriate department head in order to have the department host a show featuring your work. This may be of particular significance when your work directly relates to the subject matter of interest to the department. For instance, your documentary coverage of a native population in the South American rain forest might be of interest to an Anthropology department. In addition to the show they might want you to make a presentation to the students and faculty.

Enter Contests

There are many photography contests that you can enter but many are thinly veiled rights grabs and others are simply run to generate income from amateurs. Be selective about the contests you enter if your goal is to gain exposure to potential customers. Most contests can be found via a web search. Enter those that are directly relevant to the type of work that you do. Some might be very restrictive or follow a theme like Motherhood. Others are of more general interest. Over the years I've seen many contest entries. They ones that seem to get the most attention are impactful, sharp, contrasty, and simple. Contests often have an entry fee. The entry fee may permit you to submit several images. Submit your best images that reflect the theme of the contest. Don't feel obligated to send the number of images the contest fee permits you to submit. Don't hand over your rights. Read the rules carefully. If there is wording in the contest rules that implies you are handing over your copyright, or that you are giving unlimited rights to use your images, don't do it.

Image Leasing

Doctors and other professional environments need high quality images in their office spaces such as lobbies and waiting rooms. A savvy photographer can leverage his collection of images by leasing his art. Another option would be a lease to own arrangement in which you supply the art pre-framed and ready to hang. The customer would lease each piece for a fixed time period. Often the art is changed out during the lease period. For instance, for a one year lease there might be one change per quarter.

Boutique hotels are another potential customer for image leasing. These are small, high-end hotels often located in a city's arts district or other well-to-do part of town. They are usually heavy on design. Visit a few of these hotels to get a feel for the type of art they feature in their lobby. If your work is compatible then contact the hotel management to make your proposal.

Assignment

1. List four ways you could show work relevant to your chosen genre.

2. Prepare a plan that you would implement to show your work in one of the ways you have defined.

3. Make at least three phone calls and find out how many of the venues in your locale display art on a rotating basis. Find out how to submit a proposal from the ones that do.

13. Create Your Portfolio

The key tool that you as a photographer have to sell your work is your portfolio. This should be a cohesive collection of images representative of, and demonstrating your capability to shoot the subject matter of interest to the clients that you wish to hire you. In creating a portfolio it is important that you do not confuse the viewer, show your best work, and present it professionally.

Clarity and Consistency

Don't confuse your potential customers by mixing images of different genres in a single portfolio. Even within a single genre it is often a good idea to present a body of work around a single theme or sub-genre. Many photographers make the mistake of mixing genres in the hope they will impress the viewer with their versatility and ability to tackle any photographic assignment. This is not how clients think. The phrase "Jack of all trades, master of none" is apropos here. Your customer will interpret your shotgun approach as meaning that you are not really the specialist that they need for their project and that you are desperate for any type of work that you can get. Don't distract the viewer. If you don't have any client work you can show that is representative of the work that the client is looking for, then create your own projects targeted to the clients to whom you are marketing and stay within the closely defined niche that you intend to dominate. For instance, if your genre is food photography and your niche is restaurant dishes, then work with a food stylist to create a series of outstanding "restaurant" dish images. What food client would hire you if all you show is landscapes and images of birds?

Be Critical

Show your best work in your portfolio. Be super critical of your work and the work of those with whom you collaborate in the production of your portfolio. You can be nice and be a perfectionist. You must instill the same sense of perfection in your assistants and collaborators that you yourself have. Many (most perhaps) assistants have yet to develop an eye and appreciation for quality. That's one reason they work for you. You are training them. Even an experienced assistant might possess only the level of precision that was expected by former employers. Praise exceptional work. When your assistant knows what you expect to happen next and has what you need before you ask for it, oil that well performing machine with praise for a job well done. Criticism with no reward for perfection leads to cynicism.

There is often an attitude of "good enough" among those with whom you collaborate. Stress the importance of perfection in your portfolio images by showing how their best work proves their talent in your images. Give your collaborators the same praise you give your assistants for superior performance.

Plan Carefully

Everything that goes into the success of your portfolio shoots should be well planned in advance. Don't leave anything to chance or luck. Try to minimize any post processing by getting things right during the shoot. Your goal is to not only produce a great image for your portfolio, but to develop and hone your technique in order to have flawless execution for your client work. In a real shoot you will rarely have the time or opportunity to fix things after the fact. Make your plan and then execute that plan. Use a checklist to make sure that you have everything you need and everything is set up according to the plan. Then process to perfection. Some things are out of your control during the shoot and some post processing is inevitable, but with good planning that work can be kept to a minimum.

Presentation Formats

Your portfolio may be presented in an electronic format or in print. Nothing beats a well made print in the hands of a customer. If you present your portfolio on a website then use a site or subdomain dedicated to that genre or at least a section separate from your other work. Some photographers use image sharing sites like Instagram. This is fine and can be preferred for certain buyers. Web delivered content should be tested to verify that it works for all browser flavors and on mobile devices such as iPads.

Print portfolios are usually presented in person and can be in loose or mounted print format or in a book. Some photographers create a book containing their portfolio images using a print on demand publisher like Blurb, and then send a copy of the book to their pre-qualified prospective clients. Others create a large four color postcard with images on the color side and contact information on the other. Those work well for getting your name out to a large number of potential buyers while keeping your marketing costs down. Try to find the name of the best person with whom to make your initial contact by calling the company and asking or by researching on the company's website. Sometimes a general Web search can turn up the name associated with a role, for instance when someone lists their employer and role on LinkedIn. Don't send marketing materials to a generic title such as "Art Director". Take the time to find out the name of the art director and address it to her.

Assignment

1. Create an assignment that results in work representative of the images you would like to produce for a client.

2. Make a list of those best able to help you produce the images for your assignment. See how many of the people on your list are willing to help you with your portfolio shoot.

3. Make a list of props you need to pull of the shoot. Acquire those props.

4. Produce a shot list of all the shots you want to create for your shoot. Include diagrams that describe how each one will be shot.

5. Coordinate a schedule with your collaborators and hoot the assignment.

6. Produce images for your portfolio from the assignment.

15. Prepare A Quote

Let's look at a typical sales scenario that photographers experience. It might begin with a phone call or email asking for a quotation on an upcoming project. The question might be of the sort, "How much do you charge to shoot a wedding?" or "How much would it cost for product photography for an Amazon page?" Both of those are wide open to interpretation. Except for simple jobs it is not advisable to provide a price quotation without carefully considering what will be required in order to meet their needs and fulfill your obligations. You can't do this without a clear understanding of all of the requirements associated with the assignment and it is highly unlikely the person making the inquiry will be able to provide that information on an initial contact.

Once you have learned the right questions to ask you can start to drill down into the customer's requirements. Over time you will develop a set of questions that you will typically ask. Some customers will provide a detailed quotation request, in which case most of your questions should be answered.

Do not provide a price quotation without a complete analysis of all factors associated with the assignment. If you fail to adhere to this rule and give a ballpark number, that number is what will the customer will remember and try to hold you to, not your qualifying statements. Get as much detail as possible from the person making the inquiry. Think about the implications of the requirements that your customer has stated as well as the unstated requirements that you might know exist based on your prior experience.

 Emergencies that require rapid production should always result in extra charges. For instance, a lab that produces prints for trade shows might have a five day delivery time, not including post production retouching and other tasks. A two or three day rush delivery might result in a 200% or 300% rush charge. These details are what can cause you to blow that ballpark figure you initially gave the client. Use the opportunity to educate your client and to demonstrate that you have a complete understanding of the implications of their requirements. Build confidence that you have the skills to execute and produce their work according to their requirements. Always qualify any quote with appropriate time frames for required deliverables. For instance, a customer deadline being met might be contingent on the performance of other vendors, each of whom will have lead time requirements. Some contingencies can be met in parallel, but some might not. Therefore, plan things carefully and make sure that your customer understands the implications of a delay in approving your bid. Never agree to begin work in expectation of approval. It's perfectly fine (and in some cases expected) that you'll need to research and get back to the customer with your bid, rather than trying to work things out over the phone. Even a simple assignment such as production of headshots might require some investigation on your part. Things are rarely what they first appear to be.

A common response to a quote for services is some type of counter-offer or other attempt at negotiating a lower price. Some photographers feel pressured to lower their price after they are told someone else has offered to do the work for a much lower price. This is where you need to learn to hold your ground. You know what you need to charge in order to make a profit and you know the requirements for the project because you have analyzed them before giving a price. Therefore, if there really was another photographer bidding, then he either underbid the contract or didn't do the analysis, or is intending to do something that cuts corners in ways that might jeopardize the quality of the result. A better response to such arguments is to offer to cut something from the requirements in order to lower the price. An even better idea is to present three options which meet the requirements, but offer varying quality or other considerations. Good, better, best is how this is often proposed. Try to include something in your bid that shows your ability to both think outside the box and that you look out for your customer's interests in ways that your competitors might not. It might be some service that you include as part of the bid or an idea that saves the client some money. For instance, if you shoot corporate headshots and you get a call asking for a price to shoot 100 employees, you might include a makeup artist and hair stylist in the bid to help the customer's employees look their best. Your competitors will be falling over themselves coming up with the cheapest bid. Guess who will get the job? If you are targeting clients that place quality first, then you should get the assignment.

Don't be afraid to talk about money and the terms of payment. This should be clearly spelled out and understood by all involved. If you require a retainer or other payment in advance, make it clear that no work gets done until that payment is received. People will waste your time and take their time. They will often put things off until the very last minute and then ask you to make a concession on your terms because of their poor planning and incompetence. This is a huge red flag that indicates that they will be just as inept when it comes to paying you. Better to move on and let your competitors deal with them. In some cases you are stuck with billing net 30 days, such as is common for a corporate assignment. Make sure that the terms of your contract specify that no rights to use the images convey to the client until all amounts due are paid in full. Your recourse for non-payment becomes much stronger with this approach.

How Much Do I Charge For ...

The most recurring question on Internet forums for photography business is "How much do I charge?" There is usually no easy answer to the question, not that it stops folks from chiming in with an opinion. There are many factors that go into determining a fair price for a product or service. However, any big problem can be subdivided into a series of small problems. Solve each of those to come up with your answer. What might go into your calculation?

1. Your time

2. Your overhead

3. Production expenses

4. Licensing

5. Special skills and equipment

6. Adverse conditions

Your time is your most valuable commodity. The time you spend working with a client on a bid, pro-duction, post-production, answering questions, etc. is time you can't spend on other pursuits. You must be compensated for all of the time you spend on your business, even if you don't bill for it directly.

Your company incurs expenses that must be covered by your customers. You have investments in equip-ment, technology, infrastructure, studio space, and other things that help your business run smoothly.

Each production has associated costs such as location usage fees, expendables, lab fees, services, etc. These might be expressed as line items in the invoice or bid, or they might be lumped together as a production expense line item. Customers often want to see the details on such charges and it's usually better not to mark this type of charge up. If you charge a producer fee for managing the production aspects then make that a separate line item in that category.

There are two aspects to licensing. First is licensing of locations, permits, permissions, and other requirements and allowing your use of a location and images of the location and people in the photographs. Second is your permission for the customer to use the images you produce. The first type fall more into the production expense category. The second are driven by the customer's intended use of the images. Customers often say they want a "buy out" because they don't want to have to chase you down in a few years and risk a large licensing expense. Don't sell the buy out option unless you are producing images that will never have any other use. Rather, work with them to mitigate their risk so that you keep your rights and they get the usage they need or are guaranteed to be able to purchase the rights they need in the future at a pre-negotiated price. Also, pay attention to the type of images involved, since in many cases the value of those images for other use in a few years may be nil.

Some work requires special skills or equipment. If you are the only person with those skills or the equipment available to service the customer, then you have a right to expect to be compensated fairly for this. It's not a good idea to gouge the customer on the price, but at the same time you have a lot invested in the skill and equipment so make sure the customer understands what goes into that part of the pricing.

Some shoots occur in adverse conditions, such as cold and wet weather. If you are in danger then you need to be compensated fairly for this and you need proper protective equipment to mitigate the risk of injury to yourself, your crew, and your equipment. In some cases the equipment is your responsibility and in others it is the responsibility of the client. In either case, as part of the initial research, determine who is responsible and make sure that the details are included in the project agreement. Never let a client put you in a dangerous situation without your understanding of the risks involved and safety measures correctly implemented. Make sure that whatever insurance is in place protects you and your company, not just your client. It's possible for an insurance company to pay a claim to a client and then sue you to recover what they paid the client. Your business insurance agent can be a great asset in keeping your risk exposure under control.

Summary

There are many factors that go into calculating a bid for a project. Never give a ballpark estimate without knowing all of the details regarding the assignment. Make sure that your bid covers contingencies that might arise through events out of your control. Be safe.

Assignment

1. Create a bid to shoot 100 employees at the Acme Industries corporate headquarters. The company will need one 8x10 glossy photo of each employee and one 600x800 pixel jpeg image of each employee for the company website. They will need everything delivered within two weeks after the shoot. The images should be retouched. They want the employees against a light blue background.

16. How To Close A Sale

The best place and time to make a presentation and close a sale is at an in-person meeting between you and your client. There are subtle nuances of expression between people that can't be seen over the phone or by email, and which assist in the sales process. You can obtain more insight into a potential client by meeting them in person than by other means. Therefore, always try to arrange at least one meeting with the stakeholders who have the most influence on approval of a project.

Be positive during your meeting by offering your support for the customer's choices. Even if you disagree with some of those choices, you can offer your support in a way that guides them towards a better choice. For instance, if you are a wedding photographer and your client wants the ceremony to be lit only by candlelight, you can offer your support. "How romantic! What an original idea!", you might say. You might then guide them toward a more photographically conducive arrangement, "You know, if you place a candelabra nearby with 8-10 candles I bet we can get some beautiful images with the light."

Your goal in making a presentation is to help the customer solve their problem. Therefore, have an understanding of the problem that they are trying to solve and their pain points. Address those points in your presentation. Differentiate yourself from your competition by providing some insight or unique approach to solving their problem. For instance, you have been asked to bid on a tableau photograph for a drug abuse education campaign. You might include in your bid the services of a consulting expert on drug counseling in order to gain an accurate portrayal of the scene you intend to create. When your customer compares your bid to that of your competitor your depth of understanding of their problem will become apparent.

Show enthusiasm for their project. A client often operates under some doubt as to whether they are doing the right thing and spending their money wisely. Being supportive and showing your enthusiasm for what they are doing is much needed psychological hand holding.

These same rules apply however the presentation is delivered, in person, over the phone, etc. State the reason you are making the presentation. Follow the key elements of who, what, when, and why that will bring those unfamiliar with the project up to speed on why you are giving the presentation.

Give your recommendation to fulfill the requirements stated in the customer's request for quote. For every key element in your presentation provide the rationale for your approach. Likewise, give your rationale for not taking a different approach, if appropriate. Discuss the advantages and disadvantages of each approach, particularly if you think there are stakeholders favoring an approach that you don't think is appropriate for the project. It sometimes helps to provide the analysis prior to stating your recommendation. This circumvents those stakeholders from interrupting your presentation. You might be able to knock the competition out of consideration without naming them explicitly by referencing some key process or approach that they use and the faults with that process.

State the price & payment terms along with any contingencies that may be at play. Present the alternatives you might recommend to reduce cost or provide an even better solution at higher cost. This is the typical good, better, best scenario.

At the end of your presentation, or after key points, ask if there are any questions. Silence is golden; often a question will arise after a few seconds of silence, so give folks a few seconds to ponder what has been said so that they can formulate a question. Anything that facilitates a connection between you and your customer is a good thing. A discussion strengthens that connection. In some cases there are unreasonable people in the room that you have to deal with. Rather than take a defensive position it is more productive to ask probing questions to try to get to the basis of that person's objections. Some issues can be tabled for further analysis. Don't promise what you don't intend to deliver in order to placate the person raising the issue. Table the discussion and try to resolve it at a later time. This might involve a follow up conversation to look at the issues and alternatives and propose a solution that resolves the concern.

After the question and answer session, you are ready to start closing the sale provided there are no contingencies blocking a decision. At this point you can ask the customer how they would like to move forward, or you can tell them how they can move forward. Make sure the terms have been stated prior to this call to action. This way the customer knows the requirements for doing business with your company. Try to establish specific action items as a result of the meeting. These might be items for you to address before a final decision is made, but you also want to establish a clear path to who is making the decision, when it will be made, and when the next contact will be made. It's always better for you to be the one responsible for the follow-up contact since clients often get busy with other projects and put off contacting you even if you are being given the assignment. You want a specific date when the decision has been made and a contact to get in touch with to find out if you have the assignment. If there are still open issues and you know there is a time constraint then make sure that you provide the decision makers with specific dates beyond which any additional charges might accrue. Notify customers a few days before these critical dates in order to provide additional motivation to close the deal.

Don't offer discounts. Instead, offer alternatives. Often a potential client envisions themselves as a remarkable negotiator capable of reducing every vendor down to the lowest possible price. Learn to recognize this behavior. When you start giving in and lowering your price you invite further attempts at lowering your prices, besides giving the impression that you were overpriced to begin with. Don't do it. Instead, come up with an alternative arrangement that lets them have the requested discount that cuts out something they would be paying for in the full quote. Anything you do which compresses the shoot into a shorter time must be balanced with constraints on the client to have their collective ducks in a row. This is a bad idea when you know from observation that the client is not well organized. Put your quote together with these observations in mind and try to construct your quote in a way that there are obvious things you can remove to lower the price that don't have too great an impact on the final result. You know your cost of doing business, and that's the basis of your prices. Be willing to walk away from a deal. Be willing to say No. And don't take a job that will cost you money.

Assignment

1. Prepare an outline for a presentation you would give to one of your clients.

2. Create a client brief that describes a project that you might shoot.

3. Referencing the brief in #2, alter your presentation in #1 to fit the brief. What can you add to your presentation that is not covered in your initial presentation that addresses some aspect of the brief?

17. Production

Production is the process of executing a concept with the goal of meeting the requirements for one or more deliverables of a project. There are multiple aspects of the production process. The shoot requires development of a plan or detailed guideline by which the deliverable will be met. The plan must be executed. The deliverable must be presented to the client and any required post-production work is performed to assure conformance with the deliverable specification.

Plan the Shoot

Your contract with your client should specify the requirements that are being met and should also contain the criteria, the "metrics for success", that can be objectively applied to determine whether those requirements were met. The contract should also cover contingencies and how those should be managed. For instance, if the client is expected to supply a makeup artist from 8 AM to 12 Noon and she doesn't show up, what happens then? Is there a process for finding a substitute? The more contingency planning you do on the front end, the more smoothly things will work on the day of the shoot. You can even create a simple flow chart showing what will happen during any planned contingency so that you can smoothly follow the alternative scenario. Things can go really well when you have such a plan. On the other hand, folks can fall apart like a cheap suit when an unplanned contingency occurs, especially a large production where a lot of money has been spent.

Make sure that roles and responsibilities are clearly defined. It must be understood who is responsible for which aspects of the shoot, which deliverables are expected prior to the day of the shoot, etc. Create a timeline and on that timeline mark the points where a deliverable is due and who is responsible. Make sure contingencies are spelled out. Map the contingencies on the timeline and make the important contingencies stand out. The production assistant should verify in advance that the deliverable will be met in case there is a contingency plan that can be executed to deal with a delay. Often a contingency plan requires additional time and it's better to know in advance of a problem in order to implement the alternative plan. What happens when a responsible party doesn't meet his obligations? Some people will tell you everything is fine and the deliverable will be met up to the point that it's not. This is why you need to establish an action plan for each failed contingency, even if it is not spelled out in the contract. You will soon learn whose word you can trust on a project and work to replace those people you can't trust with those you can.

Develop a checklist for each process that you will follow in execution of the contract requirements. This helps assure that everything is done in accordance with the plan and that you don't leave out critical steps, such as forgetting to gel a practical in an architectural scene. A simple error can result in an expensive effort to correct a resulting problem. Checklists may also have contingencies, e.g. a failed battery check may have a process for procuring new batteries and that process might need to be executed several days before in case it takes a couple of days to procure replacements. Some expendables such as specialty batteries have longer procurement lead times.

Adjust your planning to the task at hand. There is little reason to spend four hours planning something you are doing on your own time that will take a few minutes of your time to complete. It is when the project involves other people, a lot of resources, or cannot easily be repeated that you need to commit much more time to planning. Even nature photographers need to properly plan their projects. Their "contract" might be with themselves, but the last thing you want to do is spend money on airline tickets and rental cars to arrive at your destination with a bad camera battery, no replacement, and none to be had within a hundred miles.

Shoot the Plan

Now that everything has been planned and the pre-production has been followed without issues it is time to run the final checklist. For location shoots you should load your equipment according to checklist and use that same loading checklist when leaving the location to verify that you have everything that you brought with you. Follow the plan and deal with contingencies as they arise. Make sure that you confirm compliance with your contract and verify that you have shot everything required under the contract terms. Review this with the client if at all possible. If an exception or change occurs due to an instruction from your client, make sure your client signs a change order or other acknowledgement when this occurs, or this may be held against you later at invoice time.

Weather is often an issue with outdoor shoots. Talent and assistants should be booked with this in mind. A shoot scheduled for several days might include a weather day. Make sure this is covered with your client if it appears to be a risk for your project. The degree of risk is dependent on the type of image as well as the character of the light and scene expected in the final images as well as the typical weather one might expect at the location.

Presentation

The genre will often dictate the output format for a deliverable. For instance advertising images might be presented as projections during a client meeting and wedding photos might be images on a DVD disk. One must be careful with the delivery of images in some instances to mitigate the risk of theft of your images. For instance, wedding images might use watermarks and be presented as low resolution images, whereas an advertising client might know better than to attempt to use an image without first obtaining rights to use the image. Whenever you deliver digital images to your clients you should be certain to place accurate metadata in those image files. That metadata should include ownership and copyright information. Leave no excuse for anyone to claim an inability to contact the owner as a reason for stealing an image. We never know when the copyright laws might be changed to present such a loophole to those who steal images.

Use a limited selection period for customers to determine which images they would like to use. In many cases your contract may specify pricing information for which your underlying basis (your cost of production) is subject to change. Limit your exposure and let your contract specify when your client must complete their obligations, similar to your contingency planning prior to the shoot. In some cases you may want to keep the images available for online ordering indefinitely, in which case the contract may specify a term during which you wish to offer prints at a set price, with the option to pay the market price afterwards.

Post Production

 It is usually a good idea to hold off on post-production work until the client has selected which images are to be used. Make sure that you get your client's sign-off on any changes to the original order and contract. Post production may involve any number of tasks such as retouching, resizing, mounting, framing, etc. One might classify as post-production any work following the shoot that directly impacts a deliverable in some way. Note, these are not strict interpretations, they are just useful in classifying where an activity is taking or will be taking place.

Assignment

1. Create a sample project of the type you might work on.

2. For the project you created, write a plan for the shoot. Don't forget to include how contingencies will be handled.

3. Try to think of things that might happen that prevent the successful completion of your planned shoot. Are you protected by your contingency plan? Why or why not?

4. What post-production might be required in your project?

18. Orders and Delivery

The ultimate goal of your photography business is not to get assignments. You goal is to complete assignments. An assignment is not completed until you have delivered a product to the customer and you have received payment for your products and services. Choose the vendors that you use for production services carefully. Their performance is ultimately your responsibility. Degradation of image quality over time, failure of albums, mounting systems and substrates, and similar risks should be taken seriously because they can have a direct impact on the reputation of your business. When you deliver your products, do so in packaging that reflects your quality standards. Always include a packing list so that a customer knows what should be included in the order. Use the delivery as an opportunity to remind customers of their obligations regarding care of images and licensing restrictions.

Outsourcing Print Production

Most photographers who deliver prints to their customers will outsource the production of those prints to a professional lab. It is important to understand what goes on behind the scenes at a lab, what is expected of you as a customer, what you should expect of the lab, and your opportunities to upsell your customer with mounting and finishing options.

The Truth About Labs

I've said many times over the years that photography is one of the glamour professions that attracts people willing to work for small change. Many of those people work in color labs. Although many lab employees are technically competent there are many people working in labs that have absolutely no respect for the quality of the product that they produce. This attitude extends all the way to the owners of the labs who will often implement cost saving measures that reduce the quality of the output while putting the longevity of the product at risk. For instance, the lab might reduce the replenishment rate of chemistry to save a tiny amount on each print produced, which may have the effect of reducing print life and color accuracy of prints. Another lab might use third party inks in their inkjet printers which have an unknown color life compared to the inks from the printer manufacturer. Those prints might start to fade in a shorter time whereas if they had been printed with the manufacturer's inks they might have a life expectancy of decades or more. This isn't much of an issue for commercial work but it is for fine art images which are expected to maintain color stability for many years. When ordering a scan of a negative you might be offered a very expensive "drum scan" when in reality your negative is scanned on a cheap flatbed scanner. In many cases the management fails to maintain the equipment that they use. I've seen this many times in the past few years where a lab processes film grudgingly and fails to maintain the film dryer, resulting in embedded dirt in the negatives which can be very expensive and time consuming to retouch. Don't think that these types of issues have gone away with the emergence of digital photography and printing. They haven't. They have simply been replaced by new issues and concerns. Many photographers still have their digital images produced as analog prints, for which the chemistry issue is still a factor. But simply put, if a lab sells cheap prints there is a very good reason why they are cheap and you probably wouldn't approve of the reasons. On the other hand, high price is no guarantee of quality. You must perform your own due diligence and asking for recommendations from others is only one step in the process.

Any lab that you consider using should be very open about their standards and controls. You should ask them about the brands of materials they use down to the specific brands of chemistry and inks they use, brands and models of equipment they would use to produce YOUR work, what guarantees they offer in writing, their quality control process for final products going out the door, and a clear statement regarding the process control standards that they follow. If you can get a tour that would be optimum.

Take notes, then do your research. If they tell you they use a drum scanner and you later take a tour, get them to show you the drum scanner. Do they have one? Does it looks like anyone has used it lately, e.g. is it covered with dust? Are the employees wearing gloves when handling customer work? Do the employees look like they care about what they are doing? Do the brand names of products in the lab match what you were told are in use? Your goal is to establish the credibility of management as well as assess the character of the employees. Another hint is the manner in which customers are treated. Does the counter help act in a condescending manner to customers? Are they helpful? Do they know anything about the products and services they sell? Does the entire lab look clean and modern? How does it smell? A lab that smells of chemicals is a bad sign. It indicates that the owners do not properly vent their machines, putting their employees' health at risk. If they are so callous with respect to their employees what does this say about their commitment to their customers?

Types of Output

Most photographers sell either digital images or prints as the final product. Prints are most often printed on a substrate of paper, metal, plastic, or cloth (canvas). Printing is typically by inkjet, dye sublimation, or chemical process. There are some niche processes such as platinum/palladium and wet plate collodion, but we won't cover those here since they are usually processes the photographer will be performing and have complete control over. Pricing of output might be by the square inch or square foot, or it may be per specific traditional print sizes such as 16x20. Most print production is done using a printer with a roll of paper which might come in a 40-60 inch width. If you order multiple prints this can be a rationale for asking for a discount on your order since the order can be gang printed. Don't be afraid to ask your lab for a discount on a large order. It's done all the time. Paper comes in various finishes. Glossy paper is often used on commercial projects. Matte or semi-matte is often used for portraits. Canvas is another option for portraits and some art photography and works particularly well for large prints. One type of canvas print extends the image area around the sides ("canvas wrap") which results in an image that may be displayed without need of a frame. Although rather trendy right now, the images are not protected and the longevity of an image of this sort is in question. Treatments such as UV coatings are available to protect the image and offer a potential upsell to your customer.

Prints may be mounted and this offers additional upsell opportunities. There are many methods for mounting prints. Small prints may be mounted to museum board using archival tape made for this purpose. Mattes come in traditional print sizes or may be custom cut for the print. The matte is then attached to the museum board with linen archival tape. With prints of larger sizes this means of mounting becomes less dependable and the use of other mounting methods is more prevalent. For instance there are cold mounting systems that use an archival adhesive for mounting prints to a substrate such as Gator board, Foamcore, acrylic, metal, or other material. In some cases a clear adhesive is applied to the front of a print and the print if face mounted to a clear substrate such as acrylic, and sometimes sandwich mounted with the print between substrates. A mounting system is then glued to the back for hanging. Mounting and other additional treatments can be very expensive and are an excellent means of increasing your total sale, however be sure that you build in sufficient margin to be able to handle an error on your staff's part or other incident that results in you having to cover the cost of having to completely remake the product. Communication with lab personnel is critical. Make sure that everything is described in writing exactly what work is to be performed. If time is critical to your customer your lab may use this as an opportunity to charge 100% or even 200% rush charges. Therefore, plan your project carefully so as to leave sufficient production lead time and be sure to allow for errors that result in a redo. Much of the lab work is time consuming and your emergency can't make those processes any faster. For instance your order might be for 100 20x24 images. An inkjet printer might print a few inches per minute. Do the math. Then add time for cutting, trimming, mounting, etc.

If you intend to sell mounting solutions with your images then you need to understand the technology as well as the potential pitfalls. For instance, certain materials should not be combined or may produce less than optimal results, such as face mounting some inkjet papers. If you use separate vendors for printing and mounting, be aware who has responsibility in the event that damage occurs during mounting. Sometimes the lab will discount a remake, but this is less likely if the lab offers the same mounting solution and you chose to use another vendor, in which case the vendor doing the mounting would be responsible. This also has an impact on delivery times. For instance a lab might charge 300% for a next day rush of an image. If your customer is expecting delivery for an event and a vendor damages the work, then someone has to cover the cost of the remake. Plan for contingencies. Also, carefully inspect work before you leave the premises of the lab or any vendor working on your order. Review the condition of an item when you leave it, for instance "Let's take a look at it to make sure it has no damage." If you are asked to sign something when you leave the work, add a comment at the bottom saying something like "Work inspected by {name of their employee} and me and no flaws when left for mounting." This is very useful if the vendor's employee damages your work and then claims that it was received damaged. Likewise with work leaving a lab. You should always thoroughly inspect an order even if the lab has been careful to wrap it up neatly. Don't leave with an item without first inspecting it for flaws. Never forget that labs often employ people who will decide the work is "good enough" even when it has flaws. Don't accept shoddy work.

Quality Levels

Note that some labs offer work of varying degrees of quality at different price points. This is based on how the work is to be used and the degree of the importance of things like color matching are to the final result. For instance the lab might distinguish between a *fine art quality* and *commercial quality*, the former having much more critical standards than the latter. You will pay extra for better quality, of course. Minor flaws and color mismatch might be deemed fine for commercial grade work. Find out what standards apply before you place the order. Ask what error margin is permitted for print sizes. You might be surprised to find prints trimmed smaller than the size your ordered. Likewise for finished products. For mounted products ask what the remake standards are for mounting defects as well as the time to remake items found defective on delivery. You are, in essence, negotiating a contract and a contract should clearly specify what happens when things don't go exactly as planned. The more of this that you establish clearly up front, the less wiggle room you leave the vendor to try to get one over on you when there is a problem with your order.

Flaws

There are many commonly encountered flaws in lab production. In the days of film photography there were potential issues in the processing of the film as well as creation of prints, all the way to the mounting process. Film flaws associated with processing were often hard to detect and the blame was typically assigned to something the photographer did like leave the film in a hot car or expose it to X-rays. However, an out of control chemical process could actually have been at fault and caused by chemical contamination, incorrect replenishment of chemistry, failure to control process temperature, and other causes. Prints are often found with flaws such as roller marks and scratches from printing machines, poor color correction and density control, incorrect size, and damage from mishandling such as kinks and creases. If you leave artwork for copying or reference it is subject to damage from mishandling and the same precautions regarding notations about the condition on the piece on any agreement form should apply. Note that labs often have some boilerplate disclaimer absolving themselves of any responsibility should your work be damaged. In some cases adding a note to "be very careful with this work" may serve to act as a modification to the agreement. Ultimately a valuable work should be covered by insurance and claims resolved between the entity that dam-ages the work and the insurance company paying the claim. Never leave valuable work with a vendor without a clear understanding of how your risk is being mitigated. Don't depend on the vendor's insur-ance, make sure you have your own coverage and let the insurance company take the lab to court if they want.

Packaging

 When delivering finished work you need to be cer-tain that the work will arrive undamaged. Ideally it should also be packaged in a manner that reflects well on your business. There are many options for packaging your work to accomplish these objectives. First and foremost the work should be protected. Use new material for packaging. Surfaces that might be subject to abrasion should either have protec-tive covering or constrained to prevent movement. Acrylic is sensitive to abrasion which is very evident in a mounted image. Light abrasions can usually be polished out, so keeping some polishing compound on hand is a great idea. Protective material is a worthwhile expense considering the cost of replacing your work, particularly when delivery time is criti-cal. Don't let the last step in successful completion of your project end in failure by trying to save a little on packaging.

Have Pride In Your Work

It is amazing how often I see a customer given an expensive purchase in a cheap paper or plastic bag. Many business owners express no sense of aesthetics or appreciation for quality. This might be associated with the widespread obsession with cheap and free. Pay attention sometime to the number of times you hear the word 'cheap' from some folks. You can differentiate your business by giving careful consideration to how you present yourself, your business, and your products to your customer. Once you have established which products you will sell, begin thinking about the physical dimensions of those products and how they might best be handled and transported. A loose print might be delivered in a nice folder. A mounted and framed print might be shipped in a custom wooden crate. However you deliver your work ask yourself if the packaging reflects the pride you have in your work. Photography is a visual medium. The aesthetics of your delivered product are important and reflect the aesthetics you intend to convey in your work.

Custom Packaging

A key component to a complete branding approach for your business is the packaging of your products. Money spend with a designer on everything having to do with your company's presentation would be money well spent. From business cards and stationery to paper bags and boxes, a consistent look that reflects quality inspires confidence in your customers that they made the right decision hiring you. Likewise, your customer will be less inclined to suffer buyers remorse than he might if he received an 8x10 from you attached to a piece of cardboard with a rubber band.

Packaging Costs

Special packaging costs money. Take your packaging costs into account when you set your prices. All of the overhead associated with your business goes into your pricing formula. As in the previous example of the print rubber banded to a piece of cardboard, I think it should be evident that your customer is going to feel better about his purchase if he pays $125 for an 8x10 in nice packaging than if he paid $100 and received it rubber banded to cardboard.

But I'm GREEN

That's great. You can have pride in your work and appearance while being ecologically responsible. For instance you might recycle all of your company's paper and plastic. You might look for packaging materials made from recycled products and choose materials that are recyclable. Just don't make your customer feel like she's being given an expensive print attached to your trash.

Additional Items

When you deliver product to your customer include a list of what has been delivered. This is so the customer can verify that everything is present and accounted for. If something has been back-ordered be sure to make note of it in the list as a separate item. Also, be sure to note any contractual obligations on the part of the client, such as usage and copying permissions or restrictions.

Assignment

1. List the output formats you would use to deliver your work, for instance prints or electronic files.

2. Create a workflow document describing how you will create the output described in #1. The workflow should permit delivery of an exact duplicate if the customer orders another copy of the same output.

3. What measures can you take to establish your business as one that is ecologically sensitive?

4. With attention to your measures from #3, what packaging options might you use to deliver products to your customers?

19. Copyright Your Images

Protect Yourself

Copyright is an important subject of which most photographers have little understanding or a lot of misunderstanding and typically give much less thought to than they should. Being creatives, the protection of the fruits of their labor should be given a much higher priority than is often the case. Publishers and other buyers of photography use this to their advantage by structuring contracts with photographers that strip creatives of their right to their creative works. It is only by aggressively defending their rights will photographers be able to make a decent living as photographers.

Copyright conveys on the creator of a work the control of how that work is used. There is some variation in copyright law from country to country. The United States provides better protection for copyright holders who register their works. The fact that their creative works are automatically copyrighted obfuscates this fact which often works to the disadvantage of the copyright holder. Common perceptions are often wrong.

The fact that so many creatives give their work away and fail to enforce their rights has given rise to a feeling of entitlement to those who steal works.

Therefore, if one wishes to aggressively enforce their rights they need to take measures to protect themselves. The specific steps to take include registration of all works, addition of metadata to all works, implementation of processes to detect violations, establishing a procedure to pursue violations, and addition of a logo or other water mark to all published images, where possible.

Registration of works is essential as it affords the copyright holder to additional damages which make it likely that an attorney will take your case on spec. You may submit up to 750 images with a single $35 registration to the United States Copyright Office. This is a bargain considering the potential benefit. Thus one might establish a procedure to register images produced in a month or in a quarter. When registering online you have the option of uploading the images, however the US Copyright Office Web site is often too slow for this to be a practical option. Therefore a better approach is to complete the registration online and choose the option to print a shipping label for a DVD. Then create a DVD containing small size versions of the images you are registering and mail that to the copyright office. Create an extra copy of that DVD and file that along with a copy of the copyright information you just submitted. When your copyright certificate comes in a few weeks file that with the form and photo DVD. There is an archival DVD media called Millennium that is an excellent choice for archiving your copyrighted images. Create one folder for the full size images and one for the small versions and you have a complete archive of your copyrighted images.

Whenever you publish an image, place an image on the Internet, share an image with other people electronically, or provide any electronic version of your photograph to a customer or other party, you should make sure that you have included metadata that enables those who make the effort to research to find the creator of the image and owner of the copyright. The technical information is less important, the important information is the copyright statement and the contact information. There should never be a case in which the copyright owner cannot be located for those who put forth the effort to look.

If you publish images to the Internet you need to implement measures to detect theft of your images and use on other Internet websites. There are two primary means by which this occurs. One is the use of images on your Web site by directly linking to your images. The second of copying your images to the site using them. Linking activity is often detected by searching your Web logs in your host's administrative console. You will see regular requests for the same image numerous times from the same IP address. Theft by copying is harder to detect but it is possible. There are image search engines that allow you to use an image as a search term which then looks for other images like the image being searched on.

There are specific measures to take when you encounter a violation. Some measures involve forcing the removal of the content from the offender's site, while others might involve a lawsuit to collect damages. Damages can be very substantial. Therefore if you have a significant number of images online, register those images, and make sure that you regularly search for illegal use of those images. Find an attorney who specializes in copyright law and work out a process that you will follow when a transgression is detected. It shouldn't cost anything to have someone waiting on the sidelines to protect you. If you are going to file suit then you need to have a "take no prisoners" mentality and go for the maximum you are entitled to under the law. Some transgressors are hobbyists who have a non-business website. Others are businesses who have no regard for those who create the images that they steal. Selectively enforcing your copyright does not preclude you from going after any violator.

There is a law which increases damages for images registered in the United States when your logo or copyright information is removed. This is the Digital Millennium Copyright Act. This might apply when you add your logo to the lower corner of your image and someone crops it out or uses Photoshop to remove it. Discuss this with your copyright attorney.

Licensing

When you contract with a customer to provide photographs on assignment or use of your stock images, make any rights conveyed to the customer contingent on their payment in full for your services. This provides you with extra leverage in the event of non-payment. Make certain that you register those images with the copyright office. I would make an exception in only the rarest of cases where confidentiality constraints trump the leverage provided by the copyright. If possible, make any agreements that bind you to confidentiality contingent upon payment. Your attorney is your best resource for discussing this type of arrangement.

Once you establish a process for regularly submitting registrations, e.g. once per month, keep track of what is registered and to which registration it is associated. You do not have to register images before they are published but you need to register them within six months in order to best preserve your rights to the fullest extent. However if an image has been published and has not been registered within that time frame, go ahead and register since it may be useful for violations occurring after the registration has been filed. Be sure to follow the special instructions for registration of published works, which are a bit more stringent than for unpublished works.

Assignment

1. Catalog the location of the images that you would like to copyright.

2. How are your images organized? Can you find a specific image? Can you find images related to a specific subject?

3. Clean up your image archive by deleting images that are out of focus, have poor exposure, and which have poor composition.

4. Develop a filing system that you can use for your professional photography.

5. Copyright some of your best images. File the copyright documentation where the copyright information for a specific image can be easily found.

20. Employees

When you begin to be successful in your business you will at some point have to decide whether to hire one or more employees or contractors. There are a number of considerations that have a bearing on your decision to hire, and in what capacity to bring someone on board. Hiring people is always risky, so it's important to do your due diligence and be careful who you hire. Every employee has the capability to damage your reputation and business. Good employees are hard to find, and they are looking for a long term stable relationship with a company that will reward them fairly and show appreciation for their efforts. They don't want to be verbally or physically abused by their employers or by their fellow employees. They have a right to expect a safe work environment. Those are all common sense notions that anyone can understand.

If you are going to need someone only occasionally to help out on a specific project or to do work that comes up infrequently, then you will in all likelihood be hiring a contractor, temp worker, or outsourcing the work to another business. If you have an ongoing need for help on one or more tasks, then a part-time or full-time employee may be preferable. This is especially true if you have a task that requires special training or skills. Having the same person on hand allows them to develop and refine their skills. Therefore, the factors to consider when deciding between an employee and contractor should include the workload over time, the skills required to perform the tasks, and the number of available people with the needed skill set. Be realistic. Will your customers pay a rate that permits you to hire employees? Do you charge sufficiently to cover the extra expense? One reason for bringing another person into the company is to enable the company to handle more business. That doesn't work when you have to micromanage your employees. It's a combination of your ability to delegate authority as well as your willingness to hand over certain duties to someone you know you can trust to do the work. You must build into your assignments the manner in which completion of those assignments is measured. That's how you know the work is being done and whether that investment in the employee is worthwhile.

One of the first things employers think of when considering a new hire is how much the new person is going to cost in terms of salary and benefits. You can take a much different approach which is a winning proposition for everyone by setting an expectation of what the new employee will do for your business in terms of additional revenue, and then rewarding the employee based on the achievement of that goal. Most employers want to set a low hourly wage so that they know what the cost is going to be. This is, in my opinion, the wrong approach. When you set minimum standards for people they will meet that standard and you end up paying for mediocrity. Use compensation to enforce performance. When you do this you can identify poor performers early on and get rid of them. Your employees are more motivated because they know that they will be properly rewarded for increasing the company's profits. Note that there is a distinction between an increase in income or cash flow and an increase in profit. There are several means of accomplishing that goal. It's relatively easy for sales people as you can put them on commission, give them the appropriate sales tools, and turn them loose. Photographers and other creatives can be motivated in a similar way by paying them a percentage of sales. Other techniques include monthly contests with tangible rewards such a dinner at a nice restaurant, trips to conferences, and training. Production workers can be rewarded by tying their compensation to their output and materials usage. For instance, if you print your own packages then take the amount of shipped product and materials used into a calculation of a bonus. Bonuses should be paid either quarterly or annually. This aids employee retention. Often employees who are intent on leaving will wait until they receive their bonuses, so make the payment during a slow season which provides ample time for finding a replacement. Periodic performance bonuses during the year are tremendous morale boosters. Remember that it's less important how much a worker produces versus how much is produced per hour of work. Lazy and inefficient workers burn through your payroll with little to show, while generating plenty of overtime in the process. Why not pay better employees who work shorter hours and turn out more and better work wages that reflect their superior performance?

Vacations and sick leave are important. Vacations allow people to regroup mentally and help reduce overall stress. You should require employees to take their vacation time or lose it. Even if the employee spends the time at home they will at least get some time to relax. Sick leave allows employees to not worry about financial impacts in the event they have a serious illness. Some employees abuse sick leave and take it like vacation days. Others tend to never use it. Let employee sick leave accumulate year-to-year. If a long-term employee has a serious illness and is out for a few weeks that accumulated sick-leave will be very helpful, and will reduce the amount of stress in the workplace after he returns to work. Ask your accountant about rules pertaining to reimbursing employees with accumulated sick leave when they leave the company. Some companies include it in a severance package when they have to let an employee go due to no fault of the employee. Employee sick leave funds can go into interest bearing accounts until paid to the employee.

If you are concerned about employees abusing sick-leave then you can implement a policy that requires a physician note for leave over a couple of days, however that's one of those things that is not worth trying to micro-manage. If you are using performance based compensation then employees who are non-productive will automatically receive less income and therefore cost you less than your high performance employees. You'll soon see who the slackers are and can cut them loose.

Part-time, Full Time, and Contractors

Learn the difference between part-time and full-time employees. Full time employees may be entitled to additional benefits such as health insurance coverage. Know the difference between employees and contractors. Often a contractor is brought on board on a trial basis and then hired as an employee after a probation period. Other times a person is brought in as a part time employee and given full time status after a similar probation period.

In the United States the Internal Revenue Service has a fairly strict interpretation of contractors[1] in order to reduce the number of people who are actually in an employee role hired as contractors so that employers can avoid paying taxes. There are hefty penalties for doing this, so don't do it. And it should go without saying, but don't pay people under the table to avoid paying taxes.

---

1 https://www.irs.gov/newsroom/understanding-employee-vs-contractor-designation

Training and Promotions

Promote from within when possible. From a practical standpoint this means you need to take a holistic look at your business, determine the roles that you need to keep filled, establish training processes for those roles, then train your employees to be able to handle the new roles. An effective means of doing this is establishing certification programs within your business. For instance, a wedding photographer might have a training process for new photographers that has levels of Trainee, Photographers Assistant, Second Shooter, Wedding Photographer, Master Wedding Photographer. You can tie compensation to these levels which in turn motivates employees to achieve the next level. Make your training process formal, with classroom instruction, written tests, practical tests, and performance assessments. Make the levels achievable by a person who puts forth the effort, but don't make it too easy. Pride in accomplishment comes from achieving a difficult objective. For instance, a wedding photographer candidate might have a practical test where all of his equipment fails and he has to figure out how to get a critical shot during the ceremony with the backup equipment at his disposal. In addition to the certificate, it's not a bad idea to present a special reward (monetary or otherwise) to those who achieve a substantial certification level within your organization, such as Master Photographer. Make it a very desirable achievement within the organization.

Interviews

An interview tells you a lot about a potential new hire. Know the rules about the questions you can't ask in an interview, but don't be afraid to grill candidates to learn as much as you can before you hire them. Learn about their short-term and long-term goals. If they list experience with particular tools or processes on their resumes, ask probing questions to determine the extent of their knowledge. Many people will list a number of things to which they have had only minimal exposure yet claim some level of expertise. Ask questions to which only someone familiar with the product or process would know the answer.

Empower Your Employees

Empower your employees to solve problems on their own. Provide specific escalation paths for solving problems so that they know what they are expected to solve and when they should be getting approval or advice from superiors. For instance, if a customer orders a large metal print for a lobby display and the dimensions don't coincide with the aspect ratio indicated by the cropping marks, the company can save a lot of money if the employee knows to discuss that issue with the customer rather than making any assumptions as to how the matter should be resolved. Ignorance and misunderstanding of aspect ratios is a very common issue.

Make It Fun

Make your business a fun place to work. Throw birthday parties for employees, take them to lunch occasionally, and make your business a pleasant place to work. Your reward will be loyal employees who care about the success of the business because it will guarantee their success.

Employee Retention

It is important to hold on to your good employees. Working for you they increase your bottom line. They are privy to information about your business that may be of use to your competitors. Once they know what your business does to be successful it is possible for them to become competitors. It is expensive to hire and train new people. The best people know your processes and help things run smoothly. That being said, people do leave occasionally and you need to have processes in place to replace them. The keys to keeping good employees include regular raises, rewards and encouragement, a bonus plan or similar compensation structure, and a "Thank you!" now and then for the great job that they are doing.

Non-compete Agreements

 A popular employment contract is the non-compete agreement. These usually state that the employee is gaining important trade secret information by virtue of employment with your company and agrees to not compete with you or work for a competitor for some period of time. In reality these are usually non-enforceable or enforceable for only a short time period. You can run up a legal bill trying to enforce one, but in the end they are little more than a scare tactic. The key to preventing employees from being a successful competitors is to limit their access to your most important information. For instance, control who has access to client lists, vendor lists, and other important data. Avoid placing such responsibility on a single employee that he has access to all of your important data, since this could easily walk out the door on a thumb drive. Learn how to control data access on your network. Ideally, you should be able to identify those who access, or attempt to access, the important data on your network. An IT consultant should be able to set up alerts to tell you who is trying to gain access to information that they are not entitled to see. Give careful consideration to what is considered a trade secret to your company and then guard those secrets.

Policies and Procedures

Every business should publish an employee manual containing the company's policies and procedures. It should outline all policies such as vacation and sick leave, bonuses and other supplemental compensation, health care reimbursement policies, and rules of employee behavior. Establish rules pertaining to employee conduct and deal with any transgressions severely. For instance, sexual harassment of an employee should be a cause for termination. No one should be immune to such rules. Procedures are the official company methodology for performing specific tasks. For instance, there might be a procedure for requesting vacation time and another for reporting hours worked.

Hiring and Firing

Just as you should be very careful who you hire you should not hesitate to fire an employee when you realize you made a bad hiring decision or the employee violates an important company policy. Some employees are borderline cases. Before you terminate an employee who is a borderline case, put the employee on a program with a set of requirements with the understanding if they don't comply they will be fired. This might result in the employee's resignation, but it often results in the employee turning around and becoming successful in the organization. Such a program should have a specific set of achievable goals, a time frame in which the goals must be met, and criteria by which compliance could be measured. This would occur during a probation period. Failure of the employee to meet the goals within the probation period would result in termination. This type of program is only good for employees for whom performance has been sub-par. It is not intended for those who have been engaged in serious transgressions such as sexual harassment.

Retain Good Employees

Just as you should not hesitate to fire bad employees, you should do what you can to keep your good employees on board. Giving an employee a raise provides a significant psychological boost even when the amount of the raise is small. Keep apprised of the salary employees in similar lines of work are making. Also note that regular small salary increases are easier to absorb into your business than sporadic large increases.

Protect Your Assets

You should strictly limit the assets to which unproven employees have access, including information on your business and customers. It isn't uncommon for employees to steal customer lists and other data to use when they leave and start a competing business. If information can be segmented in a way that makes it less useful by itself, but still permits an employee to perform an assignment, then set up your business process to implement that strategy. For instance, if you have a database containing customer information, that database may be configured so that each user has a particular type of access, such as read access to certain tables and no access to others. If an employee is only given access to the information needed to perform a task and there is no way to easily extract large volumes of raw data, then you are better protected against employee data theft.

 Protecting your assets extends to the physical assets of the business such as cameras and lenses. Every employee should be accountable for every asset that is used on an assignment. For instance, an inventory of equipment sent on an assignment should be matched against the equipment brought back, including serial numbers. It's up to you how you should handle a loss. Sometimes a piece of equipment gets lost or stolen. If it's an expensive item you might file an insurance claim. It not, then most businesses tend to write that off. A small percentage of businesses might require the employee to reimburse the company. However, employees make mistakes and many people are ill-equipped financially to absorb much of a loss. If your compensation formula takes the profit on an assignment into account, then you can automatically get a partial compensation for the loss since the employee effectively gets docked for the loss. Since it's an indirect charge it tends to be less likely to cause ill will towards the company.

It's perceived as a fair result since everyone is impacted proportionally when profits are impacted.

Training

Each employee should go through an employee development program the goal of which is to bring the employee's skills in line with what you expect for the position that the employee holds or is expected to attain. Training programs only work when there is a formal process with set times and rules regarding interruptions and missed training sessions. If interruptions in your business setting are unavoidable then you should hold those sessions off-site. There should be little tolerance for absences or tardiness. The employee's future with the business must be contingent on successful completion of the training program. If you do not have the personal discipline to make it happen then your business is going to suffer and will never reach its true potential. Consider hiring a manager who is more disciplined and give her the appropriate responsibility to allow her to be successful.

Ideally, your training program should result in a certification for a particular skill set. The employee should pass one or more tests in order to gain the certification. The tests can be a combination of knowledge and practical tests. For instance there might be a written test with 25 multiple choice questions, a written scenario essay question that allows the employee to demonstrate critical thinking, and a demonstration of what has been learned. Don't make the test too easy, but do make the certification an achievable goal for those who put forth the effort.

On completion of training give the employee a certificate of achievement. These are easily printed using your desktop publishing software or word processing program. Have a celebration that permits the other employees to congratulate the newly certified employee and build camaraderie and morale.

Temporary Help

Some tasks require specialists who may demand a higher salary than you are prepared to pay on an ongoing basis. Occasionally you may have a need for several more workers than you have employed. This is when you need to bring on some form of temporary help. Contractors are specialists in a particular field who you bring on board to perform a specific job function. Keep the "contract" in contractor by using an agreement that spells out exactly what the contractor is to do and the metrics by which you can objectively determine completion of the job. Make payment contingent on that proof. If the work product is creative, then you may want to use a work for hire clause to specify that your company owns the copyright to any works produced for you by the contractor. For less specialized tasks you may need to bring in temporary help. You may bring in family members or friends and relatives of employees,

however you will probably find the use of a temporary agency to be a better approach. A good temp
agency will screen the employees, put a crew together quickly, and take care of all the tax and other
accounting details. Often those looking for full time
employment use a temp agency to try out different
businesses and you may find someone you would
like to hire on a more permanent basis. Pay attention
to any contractual agreements between you and the
temp agency with respect to hiring their temps on a
permanent basis as you may have to pay a fee. Note
that every contract is negotiable and there are plenty
of temp agencies to choose from, so find one willing
to work with you who is not out to take advantage
of the relationship. Some amount of a finders fee is
reasonable, but be aware or negotiate such arrangements up front.

Assignment

1. List the people you would need to execute your business plan.

2. Which people would be employees? Contractors? Of the employees which would be part time and which full time?

3. Part of the hiring process involves motivating desirable employees to work for you. Write a description of your company and what you do (or intend to do) that would make working for you an appealing proposition.

4. Research policies and procedures documents used by other companies and develop your own list. List three policies that, if violated, would result in immediate dismissal of an employee. Think of three procedures that every employee should follow.

21. Marketing

Many people think starting a photography business means creating a website and waiting for the sales to roll in. Nothing could be further from the truth. Marketing is a critical aspect of running a successful photography business. Your marketing efforts must be targeted to the niche that you are pursuing. It is quite easy to blow your marketing budget on a few bad decisions so think carefully about how you can most effectively invest your money in advertising or other marketing efforts.

Market To Your Niche

Each of the specialties that have been discussed here are niches within photography, and can be further specialized into other niches. If you are the sole practitioner in a niche in your market you will become the "go to" person for that specialty. Competition becomes less of a factor and it is easier to get recommendations from other photographers in your market area and to reciprocate by recommending photographers who can shoot projects that don't fall within your niche. As your practice becomes more generic this becomes less of the case and results in downward pressure on your prices and requires more work on your part to find and retain customers. In any case there are other people who can help you with sales through referrals. One of your marketing goals is to make it easy for these people to refer you. They need to know who you are and feel comfortable referring you. For instance, wedding photographers compete with other wedding photographers, so getting referrals from them is not so easy. If you have a style that is far apart from these other photographers then there might be some cooperation. You might be the guy who shoots black and white film while everyone else shoots color digital. As long as other photographers don't offer the same service or try to undercut you by offering black and white digital services, then there is no reason why you can't cooperate. Some photographers strictly limit the number of weddings they shoot each year, so when they are booked for a date there might be someone they recommend. Business doesn't have to be cutthroat, but there are often competitors who think it has to be that way. Next, there are other vendors servicing the industry, so you should develop relationships with them. The best approach is an in-person meeting, but failing that some social media based marketing can be better than nothing. If the vendor has a blog or other social media presence then try to interact with them in a friendly way. If you see their work at a wedding but you don't have a chance to meet them in person, be sure to mention them on your own social media outlet like your blog, Facebook, or Twitter. "Joe Smay at Smay Flowers had an outstanding floral arrangement at the Smythe wedding this past weekend. Great job Joe!" Then send Joe a photo of the flowers for his book. The same strategy applies in all photographic niches. A fashion photographer might find out where a key decision maker spends time online and start interacting with her by making a positive comment in response to her recent blog post, follow her on Twitter, like her on Facebook, etc. Don't overdo it and start stalking, just provide sufficient input that when your name is mentioned it will generate a recollection of your comment. You might be at an industry event introduce yourself to her. Relationships take time to develop. If you get the chance try to ask an insightful or thought provoking question about something she has recently said or done.

Use Marketing Dollars Wisely

In the preceding discussion several techniques were described which did not rely on an outlay of capital in order to generate sales, only incidental expenses. They only required that you spend a little time and creativity in reaching those people who can help you. Some marketing requires more substantial investment of money and resources. Do so wisely. For instance, one can purchase advertising on Google and carefully choose keywords such as the city in which you market and other filters for the display of those ads. You can also limit both the cost of each ad and the maximum amount you intend to spend. When advertising on Facebook you can limit your ad presentation to certain audiences. Likewise you can limit the amount you spend. There are a number of marketing strategies you can employ that are effective and low cost. These include guerilla marketing, use of trade associations, and paid advocates.

Guerrilla Marketing

Guerilla marketing refers to any non-traditional advertising you use to bring attention to your products and services and in essence is simply the implementation of creative advertising. A series of books has been published on the subject and they are well worth reading. Some of these techniques include the use of flyers, hot air balloons, projection mapping, print ad campaigns, and memetics.

Flyers are often seen in coffee shops and other small local businesses and typically have ads for rentals, pet sitting, and other small businesses. They are widely used to advertise events like music performances. An attention-grabbing flyer can attract interest from anyone who walks by who might have an interest in your product. There are creative ways to employ flyers to create interest in a buyer who would never think to purchase services in that manner. This might be accomplished by advertising for something related to the service but which brings your business to the buyer's attention. For instance, let's say you are a fashion photographer. A buyer might never buy your services based on a flyer for fashion photography services. However, if you posted a flyer saying you are looking for a model to work on a cutting edge new look, or edgy photography for your portfolio, then include your OR code, website address and contact information, then place the flyer in a place a buyer might likely frequent, you may generate several types of activity from the flyer. First, the buyer might see the flyer and snap the QR code with her phone for later reference. Second, someone who knows a buyer or who is an influencer in some way may see the ad and file the information away for future reference. Third, you may get a response from a model who wants to do something edgy and collaborates with you, then mentions you to an influencer. The key to this is to place the flyer where the people most likely to respond or you most want to respond are going to see it. Some flyers may be directly targeted at the end customer of course. If you are a pet photographer then a flyer in a pet store or veterinarian's office makes a lot of sense.

A banner on the side of a hot air balloon makes a very attention grabbing ad for early morning commuters. Balloonists fly around the first hour after sunrise and a balloon flying near a major metropolitan area can generate a lot of interest. You would pay for having a banner printed and then a fee for each flight. Keep your message simple. A website address or Twitter hash tag is perfect and easy to remember. People driving are not typically able to write down or remember a phone number.

Projection mapping uses a high intensity video projector to display your message on the side of a building or other location. One might arrange with the owner of a building or other location to project your display. Festivals and other venues are excellent for this. A high energy video presentation can generate a lot of interest. Lacking a wall or similar surface a large white helium filled balloon can be used as a projection target. Make sure your message is contained in the visual component of the presentation since audio is often competing with noise and other environmental issues.

Print Ad Campaigns

Print ads can take various formats such as display ads, classified ads, and *advertorials*. Display ads are the most common. They typically span one or more columns in a publication or a section of a page such as full-page, half-page, quarter-page, etc. Size is expressed in column inches, which is the height of the ad in inches multiplied by the number of columns the ad spans. Display ads usually contain both text and graphics. The goal of the ad is to catch the attention of the reader long enough to get your advertising message across, and hopefully result in some action on the part of the reader such as visiting your website, calling you for more information, etc. This is no place to become your own designer. Find a graphic artist who can prepare an eye-catching ad for your display ad. Consult with the advertising sales people for recommendations if you don't know someone already. Work with the sales department to get the best placement of your ad. Ad sales have been suffering due to other types of marketing competing for ad dollars, therefore do not hesitate to use the leverage of your business to gain as much preferential treatment as you can garner. For instance, if you are a wedding photographer you might want your display ad to appear in the Sunday morning society section next to the wedding engagement announcements.

Classified ads may be sold by the line or word. You can be very creative with classified ads. Instead of simply listing your services and contact info consider something like a puzzle in which you reveal a clue each week and present a prize to the person who solves it. Post a probing question then direct the reader to your website for the answer. Place a different ad each issue and if you provide interesting content readers will begin to look forward to seeing your ad.

Memetics

Do you ever wonder how a new product or service suddenly becomes very popular? Much of it has to do with the way ideas spread and the science of memetics can tell you much about the way this works. It can be a local or global phenomena. The key to this is getting the right information to the people who tend to be influencers within a group. For instance, let's say you are working on a new niche of black and white prints on aluminum and you want to shoot portraits in this medium. It's rare and technically challenging, so you are unlikely to have much competition, if any. Look for the influencers who might be useful in your market. It might be someone who writes about local happenings in his blog. You might write him and say you are working on a new project using an exciting new technique you are developing. Ask him if he might be interested in being a test subject once you have mastered your technique and worked the bugs out. Ask him if he can think of others who might make interesting subjects, that you would like to have a show with some of your first images. Now your influencer has a lead on something new in the works that people might find interesting, and he has a personal interest in having his image made using the new technique, so he has even more to write about. He can also be instrumental in driving interest in your show, and thereby in your niche. Suddenly there will be a lot of local buzz about your work. People will want to be part of the "in crowd" and have a photograph made using the new technique. There are other ways this is done. People have been hired to hang out in coffee shops and talk to each other excitedly about a product so that other customers overhear the conversation and want to find out what all the excitement is about. On a broader scale you can use social media to achieve similar results. Start slowly and begin building interest among key influencers, then announce a major breakthrough. A common theme is for someone to start writing about a product they are trying to develop. They ask questions. They report on the problems they encounter and how they overcame them. Interest builds. Then finally the product is available, but only a few at the start. "Limited availability" is often a key ingredient and getting a spot on a long waiting list means you were one of the first people to discover the new thing everyone is excited about.

Trade Associations

Many photographers join trade associations that represent the business that they are in. However, there is a different approach that can be effective in increasing your market share. Join the trade associations of the customers to whom you would like to sell your products and services. For example, if you are an advertising commercial photographer, then you should belong to trade associations or industry groups to which the folks working for the ad agencies belong. The people you meet at these association meetings are not your competitors, they are your potential customers. Use your time attending these meetings to learn what they want in photography, what opportunities there might be ahead, and make yourself recognizable so there is a connection when your proposal or portfolio hits their desk. Folks at trade association meetings are typically more at ease than in a work setting and may be a little more forthcoming with information that may help you in the sales process. Use the opportunity to learn the names of the key people to contact when you are ready to present your proposal or portfolio for review. It pays to name drop, so a mention of the person you met at the trade association meeting can add credibility and increase the probability your proposal or portfolio gets due consideration.

Paid Advocates

A paid advocate is a person you hire to promote your products and services to his or her peers. For instance, a photographer who specializes in high school senior portraits might hire a high school student as his "Director of Social Media Strategies" for a target high school. This person's job would be to influence other students in their decision on who they hire as a photographer by reporting on the cool things the photographer is up to, which of the popular students he has photographed lately, etc. A high end senior photographer might organize a fashion shoot at a tropical location and invite a select group of students to participate. The paid advocate would generate interest in the trip and make the selections of who gets to attend. By limiting access to only a few people the trip is considered very exclusive. A substitute teacher and other adults who the students like would need to accompany the students as chaperones. Other types of paid advocates are people who write blogs or have other social media followings who might be paid or receive products or services to review. Choose your paid advocates carefully. Use those who will be influential in your market area.

Conclusion

 In this chapter we touched on a few marketing concepts. There is much to learn about marketing and there are plenty of books on the subject. The key things to remember are to spend your marketing dollars wisely, be creative in your advertising, get out and meet as many people as you can, and leverage guerilla marketing and other strategies to access people in ways to which they are typically unaccustomed. People often have blinders to typical marketing messages so try to get to them via a side door such as people they know and their own curiosity.

Assignment

1. Design a print ad campaign consisting of a series of 10 2-3 line classified ads.

2. Design a simple guerilla marketing strategy for your niche using only flyers. Who are you trying to reach? How will you reach them? Where will you place your flyers? How will you know a contact resulted from the flyer? What will you do when you are contacted?

3. Describe how a paid advocate might be useful for marketing your niche? What type of person would you hire? What would they do to promote your product or service? What would be the success criteria by which you would decide whether the keep them or let them go?

4. Is your niche one where clients might be found through trade associations? Why or why not? Which trade associations? Does the association have meetings in your locale? Describe your action plan for using a trade association to find clients.

5. Describe how you might create a meme to spark interest in your product.

www.ingramcontent.com/pod-product-compliance
Lightning Source LLC
Chambersburg PA
CBHW060830170526
45158CB00001B/122